CONVERSATIONS WITH THE BODY

Nadege.

Conversations with the Body

The true sixth sense story of a medical intuitive

Robyn Elizabeth Welch

HODDER
MOBIUS

This book is intended as a guide to people
who want to improve and maintain their health.
If you are concerned in any way about your health,
you should seek medical advice.

First published in Great Britain in 2002
by Hodder and Stoughton
First published in paperback in 2002
by Hodder and Stoughton
A division of Hodder Headline

2 4 6 8 10 9 7 5 3 1

A CIP catalogue record for this title
is available from the British Library

ISBN 0 340 81943 X

Printed and bound in Great Britain by
Clays Ltd, St Ives plc

Hodder and Stoughton
A division of Hodder Headline
338 Euston Road
London NW1 3BH

Contents

Acknowledgments

Everlasting appreciation and love to my parents Claude Welch and Mena Penny Welch. Thanks Mum and Dad, you got me here.

And to my beloved family, my heartfelt gratitude in your growth to acknowledge my journey with unconditional love.

Dr John Walck and the Medical Doctors who know there is a gentler approach to healing.

Also, a special thanks to my clients for trusting me and showing faith to try a new method.

The wonderful ground angels who were always there when I needed them.

And to Jo Sawicki, founder of Channel Health, for her loving support.

Preface

One of life's joyful mysteries is that destiny can turn by accident or coincidence. So often hindsight shows us that chance, some apparently insignificant event or random choice has proved to be more influential than any carefully laid plan.

In my case it was a wrong number, or at any rate a phone call from a stranger with a purpose I could not fathom. But it had a powerful message.

I had already embarked upon a journey of sorts when I took the call that would lead me to Hawaii. After enduring a sequence of physically and mentally bruising traumas I was ready for change but I stood, bewildered and directionless, at a very complex crossroads. The call beckoned from the path of healing and I followed it.

My first steps were tentative and often faltering. It was to be many years before I truly trusted in the power that had been bestowed upon me with the confidence to describe myself as a healer. This was partly because the way I heal almost belies belief and it was only when result after undeniable result had amassed that I accepted my gift. But the journey has proved to be just fine and now I'm ready to describe it and share the inspiration.

During my equestrian years I trained horses with encouragement and loving whispers. Now this method has great influence in my treatment of body parts for renewed health. Extraordinary as it may seem, cancerous tumours have withered and vanished, muscular agonies lifted, aching bones realigned and deep emotional sorrows dispatched, without recourse to traumatic surgery or invasive drugs, under my care.

I am a diagnostic medical intuitive. With special, intense, vibrational concentration I am able to use focused energy for regeneration and operations, if necessary, to the human body. Sometimes my results are fast, almost instant. At other times longer nurturing is needed. But I have found that all body organs and glands are conversational, even chatty in simple form, although some are shy at first. They may have felt ignored and neglected in the past, in which case I work hard to establish trust for co-operation and response.

Even if, especially if, you're well and happy, try to remember to thank your body in general and specific parts in particular. Don't feel self-conscious or hesitant about sending a 'Thanks for helping me through a tough day' or 'Wasn't it fun? Hope you enjoyed it too' message. Body parts that feel appreciated will work harder for you – it's human nature. And prevention, we know, is better than cure. I can't demand of my readers a strong spirituality but I will say that if this sense can be nursed and developed, self-healing will almost certainly become attainable.

If at times I seem to be capable of working miracles I can only thank God for allowing me to channel benign energy. But I don't claim to have the power to fix everything for everyone. However, in my conversations with the bodies of people of every sex and religion I know that I can at the very least make a start. Mostly I can complete the work and my client will be completely released, their good health restored. Other times I simply short circuit or unravel the steps needed for recovery. The many client case-histories that follow should help you to believe that almost anything is possible, and all are well at the time of writing.

My work takes me all over the world and I marvel about the knowledge that I acquire in this swirling, whirling journey. Often something I learn in the United States can be offered to a sick person in England or Italy. But your heart is where your home is and that is where my faith resides.

They say that to experience sublime joy you must first have known deep misery. I am certain that the death of my mother – shattering for ever a golden childhood in Australia – a dismal marriage (which I cannot regret since it gave me my three adored children), the severe injuries in a road accident which gave me insights on pain and mortal fear, and stumbling and largely unsuccessful business venture, have all served to enable me to become the healer I am tody. Without this preparation I don't believe I could have realised what reserves of hope, optimism and faith I was blessed with.

Years ago, in despair, I begged God for a sign and then 'chanced' to see a willow tree on the bank of a flood-ravaged river in my beautiful homeland Australia. Its roots were exposed and seemingly tortured, yet the lovely pale shoots of leaf were in brave bloom in the sun of early spring. *Hope springs eternal*. So many clichés are grounded in real truth.

They also say that a problem shared is a problem halved.

I would go further and add that faith shared is faith doubled. Goodness, hope and healing can be hugely multiplied if it is shared. And that is why I have written this book.

Open your heart and mind to keep talking with love and enthusiasm to your body. It may not answer back, but your conversations will be healing. I promise. Enjoy.

Chapter 1

The Client

'My sister's dying, can you help her?' a woman's voice pleaded on the phone. Those three words, *can you help*, had become the centre of my life. Once, years ago, I had dreamed of being a successful fashion designer, but life is full of surprises.

'Please tell me about your sister. What is wrong?'

The caller was Diane Burke. She explained that her sister Donna had been diagnosed with Hodgkin's disease two years earlier. Since then, she'd had six operations.

'How is she now?' I asked.

'She still has a malignant tumour growing in her brain.' Diane's voice was choked but she went on, 'The doctors tried chemotherapy and radiation, but nothing works to stop the tumour's rampage or the breakdown of the rest of her body. It's heartbreaking, Robyn. Donna's only thirty years old.'

I am often called upon to see patients after medical science has done its best, but this case was clearly unusually serious. Diane Burke's story had touched me and I decided to see if I could help. Diane responded eagerly, 'I'll fly her and her husband Bob from Idaho. They can stay with me.'

We set up appointments for the following week.

When I first saw Donna I was shocked to see how weak she looked. The trauma she had suffered was obvious. She was bloated from the medications and chemotherapy had caused most of her hair to fall out. Many of her lymphatic glands had been removed in the course of six operations. Her eyes were unsurprisingly dulled from the horror of it all. No light of energy and good health shone through. We talked about her shattered dreams of having children, and I encouraged her to hold on to dreams no matter what. I always encourage clients to think of a happy future to keep their minds positive and the light on.

I asked careful questions to see whether she really wanted to live. Some people become so discouraged that they develop a death wish and attempts at healing are pointless for such damaged patients. But this young woman wanted life.

I described how we would work together. I told her that the most important thing she could do was to open her eyes every morning and say to herself that no matter what negative thoughts or feelings beset her she would remain positive.

I then taught her how to reprogramme negative energy into positive energy. 'Donna, this is a very important breathing technique that I want you to use. Mentally say to yourself, *I am captain of my ship. I am in control of my system*. Then take a deep breath through your nostrils, hold it for a count of ten, then round your lips and blow it out quickly through your mouth, silently saying, *Perfect body, perfect body*. Repeat this until all breath is exhaled. You must really mean it.'

'How does this work?' Donna asked.

'By reprogramming your mind and holding you firmly in the *now*. This moment is all we have because every instant before has gone. Nothing will ever change those moments or bring them back so we have to let them go to move on. The next second has not come and there is no guarantee that it will.'

Donna looked frightened and I spoke quickly to calm her. 'I am not being negative by saying this, Donna. Right now all seeds are sown. Any seed planted correctly in your mind will come to fruition, but you have to want that from the depth of your soul. Also, while you are holding for the ten seconds, you are disempowering negative feelings and emotions. Any time a negative thought comes in, we have twenty seconds' grace before it becomes an actual frequency in the electrical circuit of our energy field.'

Not surprisingly, I then needed to describe my work further. First, I told Donna that I scan the energy field and transport energy to repair and revitalize circuits.

'We all live in a large field of energy,' I told her. 'Sometimes that field is as large as forty feet in diameter. The human field is made up of waves very similar to radio and television ones. It has beautiful colours. Viewing your body's energy field helps me diagnose the weaknesses there. They look very much like television "snow". The thickness and darkness of the snow reveal the severity of the body illness or weakness. I will clear your energy field of negative energies and begin to set up a positive flow.

'Then I see the interior of the body and send energy where it is needed to heal and strengthen the body parts.'

There was much more to explain and Donna indicated that she was comfortable and alert. Even so I decided to explain the rest later.

We began the session by taking ten deep breaths. Then I asked her to relax in the chair beside me and soon she eased into the higher level of consciousness that my work requires. I sat next to her and closed my eyes. Soon I could see her energy field in my mind's eye.

Her field was in terrible trouble, totally snowed by the effects of chemotherapy as well as by her illness. 'Snowed' is a term I use to describe a lowered human energy field simply because if the circuit is badly affected, it closely resembles a blurred and snowy television screen.

The left side revealed Donna's heart, bronchial area, lungs and upper vertebrae. The right side showed the tumour, glands, liver, pancreas, spleen, adrenals, kidneys, colon and lower vertebrae.

I found several anomalies throughout her field so I cleared and strengthened those energy circuits. The work was so intense that I needed to take a short rest and looked over at Donna. She was deeply relaxed and silent. I was pleased to see her so still. I don't mind if my clients ask questions during sessions but if they are very talkative it shows that they are not truly relaxed.

I shut my eyes again and entered the crown of her head. My first port of call was the pituitary gland – one of my favourite body parts. Donna's was the most pitiful pituitary gland I had ever encountered and it pulled away from me as I approached. This told me that Donna had probably been a shy, retiring child. It also indicated that medication had affected it.

The little gland seemed to be saying, *I can't go on. I can't cope.* For the first time I mentally spoke to a body part saying, '*I am here to help you. I will give you energy. I will get you well. Come on, you can do it, you can do it.*'

The gland seemed to like being talked to, which surprised me a bit. I had once trained horses and talked to them in the same way. Now here I was talking to this pituitary gland with encouraging words and warm surges from my heart, the only difference being that instead of giving tender pats, I was infusing pure loving energy.

I might not have been surprised by the state of Donna's pituitary if I had known that she'd had little love from her parents as a child and had carried this baggage into adulthood. She had also slept on electric blankets for most of her life. The combination of negative emotional energy and an overload of electrical energy had broken down her energy field over time.

Next, I went deep into her brain. Here I looked at a certain molecule that to me represents the immune system. If cancer is active in the body, this molecule will be sloping instead of straight. It will also be surrounded by fluid. Believe me – I can see such things. I endeavour to straighten, strengthen and dry out this area and work on this in every session. Donna's was, as expected, in a shocking state. The lymph glands at the base of her crown also needed strengthening. The cerebrospinal fluids in her head were not flowing freely and her brain was receiving a powerful but uneven electrical flow.

I kept sending her a strong ray of energy as I scanned. Then I saw the tumour, approximately 2 inches long, on the right side of her brain stem. I knew how to bypass it during this session and continued scanning and sending energy to the surrounding area, working through her eyes and sinuses. I work hard on clearing the sinuses . . . they must be clear for me to check their electrical connection to the brain. I then checked her mouth for dental problems, searching for bacteria in her gums that could have come from root canal fillings, amalgam, silver fillings or decay. Her mouth was fine.

But Donna's remaining lymphatic gland system was in terrible shape. My heart ached for the tiny glands that had survived those six operations. They looked like sad, bedraggled little soldiers, exhausted from the battle. I gave them love, understanding and energy.

Her bronchial tubes showed thickened tissue, traumatized from the medical treatment, and her lungs looked black on the outside. 'Donna,' I said, 'I'm not happy with the state of your lungs.'

'I know,' she replied solemnly, 'they were burned with the radiation treatment.'

My God, I thought, *what this poor young woman has suffered. No wonder her body set up a tumour. It wants out.* Tears filled my eyes as I gently swept away the charred tissue with my ray of energy.

Her liver needed detoxing; I directed my energy deep into the left and right portals of this organ. I continued visiting the rest of her weakened body parts, lovingly repairing them.

I ended the healing session by looking at the spine. Donna's needed little work, thank goodness. My job was finished.

When I finally opened my eyes, I was pleased to see that Donna's face looked peaceful as she sat, eyes closed, head bowed, smiling. I knew she was drifting in the high levels of a deep, altered state. From the outset of my healing work, I've realized that my clients have always gone to this space during sessions where they always smile. Many tell me that it's beautiful there, filled with vibrant colours. Some have told of meeting Jesus and connecting with loved ones who have passed over.

I left Donna in this peaceful place and went to the kitchen to talk with her husband. Bob, like Donna, had a protective cloud of numbness around him, a safety zone that can enable one to go on in horrific circumstances. I thanked him for bringing her and having trust in my work.

'We have to have faith,' he said, 'we have nothing else left.'

I explained to Bob that these sessions would create a powerful shift to lift his wife from the vortex of energy she was mired in. We spoke of the emotional trauma she had endured in her childhood. He stated she had been working on it and was now able to drop the baggage of her past.

Donna came out of the altered state thirty-five minutes later. I stressed she must take it easy for a further thirty minutes until the effects wore off completely and to be prepared to be very tired for two weeks.

Donna returned the following afternoon. She had slept for twenty hours and was already looking better. As with most of my clients, the tissues of her face had plumped out, giving the appearance of an instant face lift – certainly a nice by-product of my work but not the aim of it. Her energy levels were higher.

Next time I went into her energy field and body I could see that her body parts were much improved, especially her remaining lymphatic glands. They had started to flow more strongly. I was looking forward to revisiting her pituitary gland to see whether my talk had had the effect I had hoped for. It actually greeted me and let me know that it was pleased to see me. The change was remarkable.

But the brain tumour was unchanged. I left it alone and

asked God for direction. After Donna left I went on puzzling about what to do for her and prayed for guidance. As soon as I opened my eyes at six the following morning, I thought of Donna. Early in my journey towards healing I had discovered I could work on clients' bodies from afar. I tuned into her body. It was now receiving stronger energy from her partially cleared energy field.

Words flashed through my mind: *It's time to operate on the tumour. Sever the arteries connected to it in order to cut its food supply.* Fear swept through me: I had only operated once before, two months earlier, when I'd removed a small gristle tail protruding from the end of a woman's spine. But this was a person's brain.

For the first time during my healing journey I was frightened. I came to grips with the terrifying thoughts by telling myself, *Robyn, if it's time, it's time, you would not even consider operating if the tumour was not ready for dissection.*

I said a prayer. Then I went in and looked at the tumour. I could see clearly that three arteries were attached to it. The largest was just below the centre and a smaller one was at the bottom of the tumour. Yet another lurked behind Donna's right ear.

I focused all my concentration on the tumour, setting my sights on the smallest artery at the bottom of it. I used my energy ray as a fine cutting tool and slowly directed it through. I instinctively knew how to stop the bleeding by using my energy as a force to hold it, as if I were cauterizing the artery's own energy. I held for a moment, then came away. It worked! I felt a huge surge of confidence. *You can do it*, I said to myself.

Excited now, I approached the largest artery without hesitation. Sever, hold. My heart sang as I held, then I came away, as I had before. But blood was flowing. I dived back in. Hold, hold, hold. When I came away there was blood again. *My God, where is this blood going? It will flood her brain. She'll die.*

Panic overwhelmed me. Not knowing what else to do, I went in and held and held for what seemed an eternity. To this day, I don't know how I found the intensity of energy needed. God was with me. When I eventually let go, the bleeding had stopped.

By now, I was too exhausted to tend the remaining artery. But I sensed that I had done enough for the tumour to shrink and die. After several more sessions Donna was looking and feeling much stronger. She and her husband returned to Idaho and her tumour disappeared. She is now living a full and happy life again.

I continue to see clients who come to me with a variety of ills. My work develops with every person who seeks my help. God has never permitted me to get in over my head. Client after client has stayed in touch and many have sent me letters and cards saying that their energy healing has been verified by medical tests.

Most new clients have trouble believing that it's possible to be healed just by sitting next to someone who doesn't even touch them. But I have always believed that nothing is impossible. I have discovered from my work that all body parts *want* to be well, down to the tiniest cell and atom, and I try to convey this to clients. I have never encountered a body part that could not be repaired in a person who was meant to live.

I believe that most people can heal themselves of minor ailments. I have seen many instances of this. Interestingly

enough, most clients have not even been aware of the
defect, let alone the healing that has taken place on an
automatic energy level. Those wanting to offer a healing
pathway for others have knowingly to work on themselves
daily to develop the abilities required.

My journey took many years and covered half the globe.
To learn these healing abilities, I walked a path through
experiences that were sometimes painful, stared death in
the face and eventually gave up other dreams in order to
learn and grow. More importantly, perhaps, I had to give
up preconceived notions of how a body works and open my
mind to the remarkable possibility that pure energy can and
does heal.

Chapter 2

Life Is My Tutor

My life journey began five days before Christmas in a suburb of Sydney, Australia. My maternal grandmother, Granny Penny, was there for my birth and told me later that I was a great gift to my worried parents. My brother Dennis, born three years earlier, had Down's Syndrome and my parents were naturally concerned about having another child. Granny Penny prayed throughout the pregnancy and apparently her prayers were heard as I came into the world vigorous and healthy.

My mother had been a beauty queen and was tall and elegant, with thick dark hair and the facial bone structure of a model. Dad was a nice-looking, stocky man. I remember that they were invariably beautifully dressed and groomed, my mother always smiling.

How nerve-racking this pregnancy must have been for my parents! There were no prenatal embryo tests during those baby-boom years so they were relieved when Mother was delivered of me, a perfect baby. From the time I pulled myself to my feet when I was seven months old, their major concern was to keep me safe as I raced around to learn about the world.

My first injury occurred at ten months, when I tried to swing on the guardrail outside our back door. My tiny hands were much too small to grip the railing so I fell 4 feet to the path below. I may have begun my process of becoming a healer even then as I tried to make the pain go away. At the age of two, I managed to climb over our 5-foot-high fence into the yard next door, take two eggs from the neighbour's hen house and climb back into our yard with an egg in each hand. My dad promptly raised the fence another foot, hoping to keep me confined.

I developed a passion for animals and nature. Our redbrick house faced a main road where trams ran, but our back yard verged on hundreds of acres of green pastures owned by Cooper's Dairy. These acres were my playground and my curiosity led me to learn the names and habits of all the wonderful Australian creatures living there. The lush green grass became a bed for the times I lay gazing at the puffy animal shapes in the clouds. Later, my horses grazed in that grass with Mr Cooper's Jersey cows. I spent countless hours in those green fields, later training my horses for the show ring.

Before I went to school I often went next door to Mr Chalmers's place where horses came to be shod at the blacksmith's behind his house. From a very early age, I was allowed to sit on a small stool to watch and learn as the blacksmith fitted the horseshoes. I can still recall the smells of red-hot iron and painlessly burning hoof. I adored horses and could never get enough of them. It seemed that I knew them and they knew me. I remember my first ride on a huge saddle horse that had come to be shod. These magnificent creatures would teach me much I would need to know for my future path in life.

Mr and Mrs Oddy lived on the other side of our house. He was a concert pianist and I loved to listen to the music drifting out of their back door. I knew nothing then about music being important food for our energy field, but I knew it was good for me.

I was the instigator of neighbourhood mischief. My friends and I would crawl into the huge vegetable patches belonging to Chinese gardeners who barely spoke English but would chase us home, waving their machetes. My horses, who loved the carrots I snatched, benefited from my deftness at this game.

Down's Syndrome wasn't understood then as it is now, so much of my young life was devoted to protecting Dennis from the cruel remarks of some neighbours' children. My brother was a sweet person with a beautiful, kind heart. He loved to go to the local shops for the old lady who lived nearby: helping people made him feel important. Once, astride my horse, I cornered a thoughtless friend and made the horse prance to scare her until she apologized for unkind comments about Dennis. I became adept at throwing punches at any child who dared to say anything against him.

My passion for animals grew into something of an obsession. I seemed to think that any animal that was alone needed me to care for it. One day, I dragged home a huge delivery horse attached to its cart. I parked it at the front of the house, then ran inside to inform my parents that he was alone and hungry so now I had a horse of my own. The bewildered driver, who had been making his deliveries, finally came to collect his horse and cart.

My parents lectured me repeatedly that people owned these animals, but ownership made no sense to me: if an animal stood alone it needed my help.

Those early years were full of love and security. Warmth still floods through me when I remember the large family picnics we'd have at the Oak Tree, a park Granny Penny loved. Here my many cousins and I played games under the hot Australian sun and stuffed ourselves with mouth-watering cakes baked by my mum and aunts.

Mostly I remember feeling loved by my grandmother. She often spoke of her affection and I adored her in return. She was a very strong woman who'd raised seven children on her own after my grandfather deserted her. Granny Penny encouraged my spiritual growth by prompting my parents to send me to Sunday school at the age of five, at St Paul's, the lovely church where I had been christened. My parents were not devout but I loved singing about the love of Jesus, hearing the Bible stories and pasting coloured stamps depicting them in the small books given to each child. Granny Penny didn't attend church either, but she knew the Bible backwards and often quoted from the scriptures. She would make comments like, 'You must always tell the truth, Robyn, or God will punish you and will always know if you're lying.'

I took her advice to heart, not wanting to bring down the wrath of God. One day at a birthday party I asked, 'Granny, you always write verses from the Bible on cards you give us. Why don't you go to church?'

'My dear,' she answered, 'You don't have to go to church to be good.'

These words remained with me and I've always tried to be a good person.

I was eight years old when my sister Bronwyn was born. The house was filled with excitement that January afternoon when I returned from school. The baby was going to be born that night in my parents' bedroom and the midwife went back and forth to the kitchen for boiled water, ignoring me. At last, as the grandfather clock chimed nine, a baby cried and my father announced, 'You have a baby sister.' First I was thrilled. Then I was upset because she was crying and no one could stop her. I came up with a small doll pacifier that stopped her crying and I felt great joy and relief. Perhaps the healer in me wanted to soothe the little child and make her happy.

Not that I played with dolls very much – I found them lifeless and boring and preferred to dress kittens in doll's clothes. I fed them warm milk from bottles as I cuddled them. Our house was known as 'the Welch menagerie' because of my passion for animals. People often left boxes with kittens inside on our doorstep, hoping we would care for them. I considered them angel gifts to me but my parents were dismayed, rightly believing that we would not be able to find them all homes and would be saddled with them. Once I was horrified to discover my father drowning some of my precious kittens and when he said it was the kindest thing to do, I didn't believe him. After that, I hid kittens and searched for potential cat parents in the neighbourhood.

Christmas lunches could also be very painful. One year I saw Henrietta on the table, the dear little hen that had followed me like a dog, and torrents of tears flowed. The tears I've cried over animals during my life could fill a small river.

For my ninth birthday, I begged for lessons at the new English riding school and was overjoyed when my parents signed me up. These lessons were the beginning of my enduring partnership with horses. Within twelve months I was competing at horse shows. On my next birthday my most cherished dream came true: my parents gave me Daybreak, a dappled grey pony. I felt that I had four legs under me and wings to fly. Though I won consistently in the show ring, my father always reminded me to be a good sport, to smile all the harder if I was beaten and to shake the hand of the winner.

My parents were decent people with bred-in-the-bone integrity. Honesty and principles were very important to my father, who preferred doing business by a handshake. His business was dry cleaning, which gave us a comfortable living. I attended a local girls' boarding school as a day student. I could keep up with the work easily, thank goodness, as I much preferred playing outside and training my horse for the show ring.

Both my parents were very supportive of my riding and I made them proud. At the age of twelve, I became the leading junior rider in Australia. By then I had several horses and a stable at the back of our house, I felt completely at one with horses and had the ability to tame even the wildest. It seemed they always gave their very best for me.

My father was interested in natural herb remedies and treated the horses if they became unwell. The old recipe book that he used fascinated me. The pages were yellowed and the leather cover was faded and flaking from age, but it offered effective formulas for horse ailments. I would stand at the kitchen sink with Dad as he mixed the herbs with molasses, bran and oats. He rolled the mixture into large balls that would fit down the horses' throats. He showed me how to hold their tongues to the side of their mouths to keep them from biting and how to push the herb balls down their throats. I dutifully stood on tiptoe and put my arm down the horses' gullets, though I didn't much like it.

My father always encouraged bravery and strength in me, attributes I would call on time and again in my life. During my twelfth year he took me to the edge of a 60 foot cliff. Adventurous adults were known to dive from it into the dark green river below and he wanted me to try. My mother had been a champion diver and I always tried to emulate her swallow dives, but this thought did nothing to steady my nerves as I stood poised and terrified on the cliff edge. My father showed me how to clench my fists to break the water on entry. 'Go on, you can do it,' he said. 'It's easy!' He could always make things sound simple and positive.

I took a deep breath and plunged off the cliff. I shot like a bullet to the murky depths of the river, quite sure I would never be able to hold my breath long enough to reach the light again. But I made it back to the surface at last. Even then, it seems, I was in training to reach the light at the end of the tunnel — a tunnel I had to enter later to lift my consciousness above the horrors and find the strength to keep heading for that light. And even then I knew instinctively that my determination to reach for the light would change my life and those of many others.

Let's talk of the light, the life-force. It must be constantly on in the mind's eye, so to speak. Light is life. Darkness is death. That's why energy levels are low in the majority of people who live in dark, clouded places. Sun is energy. We need light in our life to survive. A major part of my work is to instil in very ill clients a positive light to reach towards, in other words, something to live for. However, if the light is meant to be extinguished, so be it. No matter how good my work, if it's time for their journey to end, nothing will keep the body here on the planet. I really think that the reason children are afraid of the dark is because their survival instinct kicks in, creating the fear of death.

No matter how mature you are, have a positive plan, no matter how modest. Try to have small new adventures constantly to keep the light on. Don't let the darkness take over, hang on to your visions, always surging forward. Don't get becalmed, movement is wonderful for your energy field. If you're physically restricted, ask someone to help you take a small journey, even if it's only thirty minutes or so. Be motivated. Self-motivation is an energy booster. Movement frees your energies. It's important to flow, therefore, avoiding energy vortexes.

Energy vortexes are like whirlpools. Very ill people need an energetic boost to be shifted from these low vibrations to the higher vibrational levels needed for healing.

During my twelfth year, I also obtained what I now consider my first clients – six white leghorn hens. One morning as I walked up the path to catch the school bus, I heard a commotion in Mr Chalmers's yard and climbed the fence to see what was happening. To my dismay, his yard looked like a battlefield covered with bloodied white bodies and the grass was littered with feathers. A neighbour's dog had broken into his hen house. Mr Chalmers was checking for life, putting an end to the birds' misery, muttering angrily as he went. I could not comprehend death. I begged him to allow me to try to save some of the chickens, so he gave me six. My parents allowed me to stay off school that day to tend my patients.

I took the battered hens into a small shed at the side of the house. I don't know why, but the first thing I did was give them all a dose of castor oil. I bathed their bodies with antiseptic and made splints for broken legs with flat sticks, securing them with ripped pieces of sheeting my mother had given me.

Five survived and went on to lay eggs. This made me so proud. They became part of my growing family of pets which by then comprised three horses, a dog, five cats, two with hidden litters of kittens, and a wallaby named Hoppy who followed me like a dog. She would even jump over the fence to follow me on my bicycle, much to the amazement of the neighbours. I also harboured a flying fox named Bat, who lived in our apricot tree. This precious little creature had fallen from his mother when he was still a suckling, so I taught him to hold a small bottle of milk with his claw hands and drink from it. He looked adorable hanging upside down drinking his formula. Training animals to do such things gave me incredible joy and, for a while, animals meant more to me than people did.

That changed when my beautiful mother started to slow down. When she began to need naps during the day, my father insisted that she see a doctor. She refused, saying it was probably only the onset of the menopause. Looking back, I feel she sensed she had cancer. I remember sitting by her feet one night in our cosy sitting room as she cuddled my baby sister. I don't know or remember how the conversation arose, but she said, 'What would you do if I died?'

'Oh, Mummy!' I cried. 'Don't be silly, you will never die.' My mother die? What an impossible thing to consider.

My father finally summoned a gynaecologist to come to the house. After the doctor had examined my mother, my father told me that she was very ill and would be taken to the hospital. As my father drove her away, she looked back at the house and I could see that she was crying.

Several days later, after she had had an operation, I was taken to visit her. I was shocked. Her beautiful face had become grey, gaunt and hollow and she was extremely weak. My father rubbed ice across her lips. I took the ice, wanting to do it for her, but she only wanted my father. Feeling somewhat confused and rejected, I was sent into the hospital corridor. My uncle, my mother's brother, was standing there, crying uncontrollably. He took me by the shoulders and told me my mother was dying. I was hit by an incredible surge of grief and screamed out, 'No! No!' This couldn't be happening. At the age of thirty-eight, my mother had cancer of the cervix which had spread to her liver.

We went home and within a few days my father was called to the hospital. I had a horrible feeling before he went and when he drove back into our driveway, I ran out to the paddock and he couldn't catch me. He was calling out to me, but I yelled, 'No! I don't want to hear it.'

Finally he caught me and held me, but I knew my mother was dead before he could say the words. There was no closure for me; young teenagers did not go to funerals then, but I mourned by myself. Her death changed my life entirely.

Chapter 3

The Depth of Responsibility

My happy, carefree childhood was over. Mother's household duties fell on my thirteen-year-old shoulders and I was responsible for taking care of my little sister Bronwyn and brother Dennis. At four, Bronwyn was too young to understand why her mother was no longer there and Dennis was not able to comprehend death, but we were all heartbroken. Our evening mealtime, which had always been a happy family gathering, became a tearful ritual.

Those harrowing suppers led me to my first meditation experiences. After my father left the table, I would take a piece of leftover bread, roll it into a marble-sized ball and squeeze it as I 'spaced out' to get away from the pain in my heart. If my father spotted me in this condition, he would quickly bring me back to planet Earth by demanding loudly, 'Snap out of it' or 'Come down from the fairies.'

Perhaps he was frightened that I was leaving my body and might not be able to return to reality. But he didn't have to worry about me. Soaring into higher dimensions of consciousness is a protective, healing experience that helps us get through emotional disturbances. To go to these dimensions is like going to a protective sanctuary. I now believe that children find it easier than adults to reach high levels of vibration because most of them are not yet firmly grounded in the three-dimensional vibrations of the Earth.

I may have achieved temporary respite from emotional pain by these meditative experiences, but no matter what I did or where I went, I could not escape the living nightmare of my lovely mum's death. I awoke every morning feeling the physical pain of her loss and was consumed with guilt for not hugging her more often, telling her I loved her and thanking her for all she did for me. How I wished I had not taken her for granted.

I hated God for taking my mother away. Granny said that she had been taken to Heaven, but I found that hard to explain to Bronwyn and Dennis when they cried for their mother's arms.

Despite her own failing health, Granny Penny walked 3 miles to our house every day to help us and always arrived with a bag of candy to cheer us up. She had always helped my mother take care of Dennis and continued to enfold him with the love he so badly needed.

My father seemed embarrassed by Dennis's condition and was uncomfortable appearing in public with him. Apparently, he felt responsible for Dennis having Down's Syndrome because he'd had pneumonia when Dennis was conceived. Of course, there was no scientific basis for this but Father never shook off his guilt.

Fifteen months after the death of my mother, Granny Penny died of a heart attack. I was devastated. My pain deepened and my burden grew heavier. Because of house-hold commitments, my cherished riding career ended and my schooling stopped too early for me to go to college. This was especially distressing because I had been doing really well at school. My mother had dreamed of me attending university, but Father brushed it off, saying, 'Girls don't need to go to university. Their role is to get married and have babies.'

The pressures of my life started to affect me. No longer a bright, outgoing girl, full of confidence, I began to withdraw. To keep my spirits up when I had to stop riding horses, I began to swim at our local pool and won the district championship. Although the water offered some healing to my broken heart, no matter what I did, I couldn't fill the bottomless pit of grief left by my mother's death.

At the age of sixteen, I was keeping house, cooking, looking after Bronwyn and sending her off to school daily, and caring for Dennis, who had also started to become withdrawn. One day I collapsed on the floor and could not 'pull myself together,' as my father demanded. Try as I might, I could not stop my tears or control my shaking. The doctor said I was having a nervous breakdown and recommended a holiday.

My father sent me to the coast with my swimming friends. This allowed me to rediscover my lighthearted side and I came home stronger and happier than I'd been in years. The doctor wanted me to get out more and mix with people and suggested I get a job. Going to work in a jewellery shop was good in one way but even more of a burden in another, because I still had a household to take care of as well as my work. I wasn't entirely on my own, however. My father drove my sister to and from school and Auntie Bernice, my mother's sister, took care of Dennis when my father and I went to work. Bernice had been close to my mother and never quite recovered from the shock of her death.

My father was under great strain too and wasn't as positive and encouraging as he'd been before. I wish he were still alive so we could talk about those terrible years. Not long after my mother's death, he started dating and soon had a glamorous woman friend. Although I had mixed emotions about it, I was happy that he had a close friend.

Soon I was old enough to start dating myself and a series of young men came into my life. Understandably, my father was very strict and set early curfews. He was afraid I'd become pregnant and I was afraid of facing his anger if I did. Although I had a normal teenager's curiosity about sex, I believed that making love should be saved for marriage.

By the age of eighteen, I was commuting to Sydney where I'd found an interesting job as a junior interior designer in a smart furniture store. The work felt easy and natural for me. I enjoyed the challenge of balancing textures and colours to create harmonious beauty. But I still had to contend with my duties at home and was very concerned about giving Bronwyn as normal a life as possible.

On the train to Sydney one morning, I read in the newspaper that trials were being held that day for an American synchronized swimming team touring Australia. I was so excited that I decided not to go to work. Instead, I went home to get my bathing suit, caught the train back to the city and headed for the harbourside to audition for the Swimming Follies. I was thrilled to be accepted. I performed nightly for three delightful months and earned a huge wage. The team manager invited me to return to America with them. My father refused to give his permission. I couldn't go against his wishes and I felt responsible for Dennis and Bronwyn so I didn't argue with him.

Swimming in the Follies led to a swimsuit-modelling job.

I was regaining some of my lost confidence, but I still suffered from attacks of nervousness. I forced myself to push through these attacks and managed to enjoy the modelling.

At about that time Dennis began to behave strangely, probably because no one had been able to replace Mum or Granny Penny in his life. After discussion with our family doctor, Father decided to commit him to a special care home. The doctor told us that it would be best if we did not visit him, to enable him to make a clean break with the family. 'They live in a world of their own anyway,' I heard him say. Sending Dennis away didn't feel right to me, but I could do nothing about it. Thank God, the public's attitude towards Down's Syndrome condition has since changed.

I missed my brother and longed to visit him. Auntie Bernice and her husband agreed to take me. Although my father had forbidden visits, for the first time in my life I went against his wishes. Dennis was obviously pleased to see us, but wouldn't speak. He was never to speak again. I'm sure it was his way of showing anger for what we had done to him.

When my father found out about the visit, there was hell to pay. He won the family arguments and that was the last I saw of Dennis for many years. I tried to convince myself it would be easier not to have him around because I'd have to explain his condition to boyfriends.

I had many dates and casual relationships and then I met Peter, a handsome Greek, whose charm and vitality swept me off my feet. He was the first man I'd gone out with who actually courted me with good manners, flowers and chocolates.

I was excited when Peter proposed. When I told my

father that Peter was going to ask him for my hand in marriage, he shook me by the shoulders. 'Robyn, it won't work. Peter's Greek family will never accept you because you're of a different nationality.' Then he paused and looked into my eyes. 'And his family will never be accepted by ours.'

I was devastated. That's how it was in Australia back then – most people believed in sticking with their 'own kind.' Again, I obeyed my father's wishes and broke with Peter.

Max came along after that and I was smitten again. This time my father agreed to our marriage, but without total enthusiasm. 'He seems to come from a good bloodline but his shoes are never shiny enough. That means his principles will be poor.'

My father placed principle above everything else, but he had no idea that Max drank too much and I kept my worry about this to myself. Eventually, my reservations and my father's would prove to be well founded, but at the time Max's positive traits overcame my silent concerns. Good-looking and polished, he was a great conversationalist. I still felt nervous in social situations and found in him things I seemed to lack myself. The youngest of eleven children, Max had been spoiled rotten. His boyish charm would have little value when the going got rough, but I didn't understand that at the time.

Max was working as a purser on a cruise ship when we met and looked gorgeous in his uniform. The old saying about women falling for a man in uniform certainly applied to me. I was head over heels in love. Three weeks after our engagement, he went to sea on an eight-month tour of duty. When eight months lengthened to eleven, I sent him an impassioned letter telling him I was too lonely and stating, 'It's the sea or me.'

Much to my relief, Max came ashore and went to work for an insurance company. I was twenty and he was twenty-five when we got married at a magnificent ceremony at St Andrew's Cathedral in Sydney, which looked like a smaller version of Westminster Abbey in London. The church is one of the most beautiful in Australia but I did not feel close to God there or anywhere else for that matter. I had not yet forgiven God for taking my mother from me. But I wasn't thinking about God when I floated down the long aisle in a magnificent gown created by Auntie Bernice. My only regret was not having my mother there.

Max and I both loved the water so we settled into an apartment in a beach suburb of Sydney called Cronulla. I adore the healing qualities and the sensuous feeling of the sea and I swam a mile every day. Bronwyn missed me and soon moved in with us. She was well behaved and Max didn't mind at all. We were very happy.

Six months into our marriage, I became pregnant. I was delighted with the prospect of having a baby, but back then there were no books or workshops about pregnancy and childbirth so I barely understood what was happening to my body. I was so ill informed that when my waters broke, I was upset because I thought I had wet the bed. It happened right after Max left for work and I frantically called Mardie, my downstairs neighbour. She reassured me that it was a natural part of childbirth. Max came home and rushed me to the hospital.

The sister on duty was reluctant to admit me because I was so small that she didn't believe I was full-term, but she finally sent me to the maternity ward. I was prepped and told by the attendant to watch the clock on the wall and time my pains. After she left, I heard horrible screams from a woman down the hall and became terrified that I would be in for an equally bad time. I pulled myself together by reminding myself that I was not the first woman in the world to have a baby. 'Robyn, no matter what lies ahead, you will not make a noise,' I kept telling myself.

My little pep talk had the desired result and I made it though my day-long labour without a sound until the final moments when I groaned as I pushed my baby daughter into the world. Jane was beautiful! She weighed only 5 pounds 14 ounces but she had perfect features, olive skin and enormous blue eyes. When I held her in my arms at last I was filled with love and pride. I was also relieved that she was normal. During my pregnancy I had been concerned about the possibility that my child would have Down's Syndrome, though it is not considered hereditary. Then I wondered whether I loved her enough to give my life for her, and was surprised to find that I was not sure that I would. If anyone had asked me that question three months later, however, the answer would have been a resounding yes.

Looking back, I find it quite remarkable that after a long, painful labour, my first sentient thought was, would you give your life at this moment for this small, beautiful bundle? I view this as the first deep thought I'd ever had about love, the life-force which had surfaced from the pain of labour. It's now a known fact that women reach a very high vibrational level after childbirth. Nature brings this about to boost the senses, especially the ears, for the baby's needs. Some women can't maintain this and crash into post-natal depression.

So I had started to seek the highest feelings of love by testing my thoughts. Knowing what I now do from scientific testing that has come mainly from the USA, I was unknowingly working to expand my energy field because the love frequency is indeed channelled through the heart.

After I was taken from the delivery room to my ward at three in the morning, I turned out the light and lay back on my pillows feeling beautiful and happy. Suddenly, finally, I could feel God's presence in the room and the walls actually glowed. Tears flowed and I thanked God over and over for the gift of my beautiful baby.

I slept very deeply. When I awoke, I was convinced that the light I had seen was Divine. I had come back to God; my anger had ended. I realized later that I'd had a classic born-again experience. In my naiveté, I believed that every woman saw Divine light after she gave birth and told my pregnant friends to anticipate the magnificent experience. None of them saw that light, but by then my friends were becoming accustomed to my viewing events from a spiritual perspective.

Soon after I arrived home with Jane, I despaired of the boring, unimaginative baby clothes in the stores, so I began to sew for her. I got such satisfaction from this that I designed and made clothing for nearby children's boutiques. My hobby became a major part of my life and I sewed nearly everything we wore, even Max's underwear. I'd sometimes work until four in the morning, eager to see the finished product.

Max and I found a lovely old colonial house that needed renovation. We went to work to restore it to its former splendour and enjoyed both the process and the results. I managed to find time to attend pottery classes and take up squash. My energy was boundless.

I wanted another baby and soon became pregnant again. Our second daughter came into the world feet first, a breech baby. We named her Sarah after Sarah Bernhardt, the great actress whose picture hung in our home. Later, interestingly enough, our daughter's acting ability led to her becoming the youngest student ever accepted by her chosen college.

Two years later, my son Aaron was born. We were thrilled to have a boy. Aaron was an easy baby to care for, somehow much less demanding than the girls had been.

When he was a toddler, we purchased an old 45-foot sailing boat named *Sea Witch* and restored it. For several years we enjoyed taking the family out sailing. Then Jane and Sarah wanted their own horses so we turned our attention to activities on the land again. We bought a few horses and I taught the girls how to ride in shows as I had done.

One day I spotted a forlorn chestnut at a knackery where horses were sold for dog food. This depressed animal was not much more than a bag of bones standing up to his fetlocks in mud on badly swollen legs. His head hung so low that his mouth almost touched the ground. When he looked up at me, the deep sadness in his brown eyes touched my heart and I knew I had to help him.

I asked the manager how much he wanted for the horse and was amazed when he said 500 dollars. He explained that the horse, whose name was Inca was well bred and he had papers to prove it. I couldn't have cared less about the papers; I just wanted to help Inca, so I paid the exorbitant-seeming price and took him home to nurse him back to health. He responded well to our tender care and within a few months had regained much of his strength and started to look better.

I was gradually becoming aware that I was clairvoyant. When the phone rang, I usually knew who was calling before I picked up the receiver. I was also able to make predictions about positive events in my friends' lives and they always came true. This led me to seek out information on the paranormal. There were few books on the subject available in Australia, but I found *The Third Eye* by T. Lobsang Rampa, who claimed to have been raised in a Tibetan lamasery where he studied the mystical arts. I devoured his books, fascinated by his accounts of reincarnation, astral projection and other spiritual attainments. I learned that each person has a purpose in this life and I hoped to discover my own path to enlightenment. Rampa believed that the path to our destiny is revealed when we open ourselves to the All-Powerful and All-Knowing. I would have enjoyed further studies on the paranormal, but had little opportunity to pursue these.

Max decided that we should move 600 miles away to a region now called the Gold Coast in Queensland, then a burgeoning resort area. There, he believed, he could do well by opening a carpet centre to cater to new residents. The beautiful house we had restored sold for a very good price so we were able to get established nicely.

It took two trips in a converted furniture van to move all our things and the six horses. Max drove the huge vehicle for a total of 2,400 miles but we were in high spirits, treating the gruelling journey as a grand adventure.

We rented a house until we could find one we wanted to

buy and found stable space for the horses close to the
nearby racetrack. One day as I was riding Inca a man
stopped me to admire him. When I told him my horse's
story, he said he was a trainer and would be interested to
see Inca's papers. I knew very little about the lineage of
racehorses, but I returned with the pedigree a few days
later. The trainer informed me that Inca was one of the
best-bred racehorses in Australia. He suggested that I obtain
a racehorse trainer's licence, assuring me that I would have
no trouble because of my background and knowledge of
horses. I'd never considered doing such a thing but I applied
and to my amazement received my licence.

Inca and I began a rigorous training schedule. In
addition to house hunting, delivering my small children
to school and taking care of the other horses, I was
rising at three-thirty every morning to get Inca to the
racetrack for training. He did very well, and, looking
forward to race day, I sewed stylish outfits for myself
complete with hats, so that I would appear as the
glamorous lady trainer.

As Inca started racing I would proudly lead him around
the starting paddock, then boost my jockey aboard, saying,
'Set your own pace, do anything you have to, but don't you
dare whip him.' Unfortunately, after a few races, Inca
exhibited a tendency to have a bloody nose. This condition
can kill racehorses, so I stopped racing him. There were
other opportunities for this great horse, however, and he
went on to glory as a jumper, representing our state in the
Olympic trials. I often wonder how successful he might
have been as a racehorse if I'd known of my healing ability
at that time.

We found a beautiful home complete with a swimming

pool and enough land for horses out back. It was perfect for our family as there was a fine school nearby.

One of the horses, Oysterman, a magnificent 16-hand grey, was starting to anticipate my vocal commands before I spoke. At first I thought it was my imagination, but this was happening on the end of the 30-foot-long lunge lead that I held as he exercised around me in a circle. At the time, I was having lessons from a famous riding instructor from England. I wanted to ask him if he believed horses have ESP, but I was worried the other students would think me strange. As the course ended I finally plucked up the courage to ask him. Imagine my relief when he answered, 'Of course they do, Robyn.' It was good to know that my psychic connection to Oysterman and other horses was not just imaginary on my part.

Whenever I had paranormal experiences, I sought verification to affirm my belief that they were real. I trained many horses during my riding career, but only four had strong ESP. Three of the four were very difficult to train because they were just too knowing. The one I was able to train to a very high standard to win at the Royal Horse shows was a retired racehorse named Charles de Gaulle. During the first three weeks I tried to train him, Charlie would do nothing but buck and rear to try to unseat me. He even attempted to throw himself on the ground to get rid of me. I kept gently telling him that I wanted him to be passive. Then one day he said, 'You win.' After that, Charlie worked with me like a lamb. I'll always be grateful for how much these wonderful creatures taught me. Nights now spent lying awake going over a patient's lack of progress are virtually identical to the sleepless nights caused by a horse becoming stuck in a training movement, when I used to keep myself awake questioning whether it was a physical or mental block in the horse or myself that was the root of the problem.

Life at that time was pretty much a dream. The carpet business was slow, but we were buying and selling land for profit, so money was not an issue. Our family was happy and healthy. Everything was perfect.

Two years later our beautiful bubble was to burst.

Chapter 4

Sixth Sense Development

I woke up one morning with a strange feeling in the pit of my stomach. I tried to shake it off, but it would not go away. As I was putting on makeup in the bathroom of our Gold Coast home, I glanced out into the courtyard and there lay a dead frog spread-eagled on the ground. I shuddered when I saw how closely it resembled a human body. Now I'm quite sure that the frog was an omen of what lay ahead, but I did not understand it at the time.

My friend Martha had asked me to take care of her four young sons for the day while she ran errands in town. Still feeling anxious about something, I put off my housework and did nothing but tend to the boys and my own children all day.

When Martha drove in at four in the afternoon to collect them, I was relieved to see her and invited her in for a cup of coffee. James, her beautiful blond two-year-old, came to the kitchen with us and I peeled an apple for him. Five minutes later, when Martha called the boys to take them home, James did not answer.

I ran to the back of the house, hoping he was not in the horse paddock. Then I heard Martha screaming from the front yard. I ran through the house towards the pool and saw her coming up from the deep end with James in her arms. She collapsed at the side of the pool. I took him from her and desperately tried to give him mouth-to-mouth resuscitation. The slime and apple pieces coming from his mouth were smeared all over my face, making me retch between breaths, but I went on even though I knew at some level of consciousness that he was dead. My husband arrived just then and phoned for an ambulance. James could not be revived; he had cracked his skull on the way into the pool.

For days I was doubled over with stomach cramps. Physical and emotional pain swept over me in waves; I was consumed with guilt for not having a fence around the pool, with self-recrimination for letting down my guard when his mother arrived. Attending the funeral and seeing the tiny white casket made it much worse. I could only say, 'I'm sorry, I'm so sorry,' between the pains that came with each sob. Martha tried to comfort me, saying, 'It was not your fault. I knew I was only to have him for a short time.'

I could not have felt worse at that time had it been one of my own children. I wore the emotions of James's drowning on my face in the form of a red rash for two years and for years afterwards I felt that part of me disappeared when he died. I never thought I'd be whole again.

I could not face looking at the pool any longer and wanted to run away to the beauties of nature to heal. I suggested to Max that we sell our house and move on to ten glorious acres we owned nearby. It was a very pretty parcel of land with verdant green pastures, mature cedar trees and a running river of crystal water cascading over satin-smooth stones. We could live in a mobile home and buy a generator for power and a water pump. I knew the children would love it.

Max wasn't so sure, but finally he agreed. We purchased a large mobile home and had it transported to our property. It had no shower, but that didn't matter; we could easily bathe in the river. The children thought that camping in a mobile home was great fun and they settled in without complaint.

We designed a lovely house and a large horse barn that we planned to build from slate bricks from a quarry near our property. We contracted with James's father to be our builder. He was a skilful and reputable contractor and, after all we had been through together, we felt we could trust him implicitly. Our contracts were made on a handshake basis. He and his wife had separated by then, which probably affected what happened next.

We didn't realize that he blamed us for his son's death. He'd seemed friendly and forgiving before, but now we weren't so sure. Many things went wrong with the construction work and we ran out of money before our house and barn were finished, so we rented a house in town. Max sometimes drank a little too much, became depressed and soon his business crumbled. We lost everything and our marriage turned into a nightmare.

Finally I had no choice but to leave so I moved with the children into an old house next door to a stable. I worked there twelve to fourteen hours a day to support the children, painting fences, mucking out the stables and exercising the horses. Max had gone into a deep decline. Although we were separated, I gave him money. After a few months I felt so sorry for him that we moved back together.

A little while later friends of ours, Janet and Carl, called to say they had purchased a renowned historical home and invited us over to see it. I always felt drawn to the magnificent house when I drove past it and had longed to see what it looked like inside.

When we toured the house with our friends, it was like a dream come true. Built in the English colonial style with a series of wings surrounded by wide verandas, it was perfect for the hot Australian climate. But as I walked through the rooms, I began to feel apprehensive. We entered a wing consisting of a bedroom, nanny's room and nursery, and Janet and Carl excitedly described their plans to transform the rooms into a master suite with a bedroom, bathroom and dressing room. As we stood in the bare bedroom, I was hit by a freezing chill that surged through my body. Along with this feeling came a vision of the room filled with lovely antique furniture. In the double bed lay the still form of a baby: a man and woman were bending over it and a nanny in uniform was sitting on the edge of the bed. They were all crying because the baby was dead. I somehow slipped into their emotional reality and was overwhelmed by incredible heartache.

The vision was so real that when my consciousness returned to my own reality, I was shocked to hear our friends still discussing their decorating plans. Moments later the chill invaded me again, even colder this time, so cold that I doubled over, wrapping my arms around myself. I was aware that the others in the room noticed my strange behaviour but I didn't say anything to them.

I could not get the vision I had seen out of my mind as we walked through the rest of the house. I didn't want to be impolite, but I could hardly wait to leave. When at last we headed to our cars, we noticed a pretty little sandstone church across the street with the door standing open. The temptation to view it was too great to ignore. We walked down the red carpeted aisle to the baptismal font. On the font was a shiny brass plaque that told us that it was a memorial to three babies who died in Mount Victoria House, aged respectively eight months, fourteen months and two years. Janet immediately guessed the cause of my strange behaviour and asked, 'Robyn, that's what was wrong with you in the bedroom, wasn't it?' I had to say yes but indicated that I didn't want to discuss it with our husbands around.

Janet telephoned me the following week. She had checked the history of the house and discovered that the original owners had lost three babies, resulting in the father committing suicide and the mother becoming an alcoholic. The next owners also lost children and the parents came to the same tragic end. Janet asked whether I thought they should buy the house under the circumstances. I told her not to buy, but by the time she and Carl called their bank, it was too late for them to back out of the deal.

We lost contact with Janet and Carl when we moved away, but several years later we heard of the incredible effect the house had on their lives. Their business went bankrupt, the marriage ended, their son became a hopeless heroin addict, their young daughter fell pregnant to a bike gang member and eloped with him. Janet became an alcoholic and Carl fell gravely ill.

They had been a marvellous family and the news saddened me. But it also convinced me that emotional frequencies that I picked up in the house were implanted in the timbers of the place and would affect anyone who lived there. Later, when my healing energy evolved, I discovered that emotional frequencies are implanted only in furniture and fabrics made of natural materials. A home should be a person's re-energizing area and it is important to keep the frequencies as positive as possible. I advise my clients to check the history of a home before buying. Usually, a happy home will continue to have positive energy, and a place where a tragedy or constant aggression took place may carry the frequencies of the negative energy for a long time, perhaps forever.

I was becoming aware that a pattern was taking shape in my life. My psychic awareness developed gradually most of the time, but whenever I suffered any physical or emotional pain my abilities took a giant step forward. I had no idea where I was headed, but my confidence of my aptitude in the field of the paranormal was growing. Why spiritual growth from painful experiences? I have evolved to the stage where I find this way of growing animalistic in the worst sense, i.e., a kick-the-dog-and-it-will-love-you-more attitude. There has to be a more intelligent way to lift the voltage of our energy field. I hope that we are now approaching a new, gentle stage of evolvement and that things will change because we will have black-and-white evidence of how our complete system operates.

Not long after Max and I started living together again, my sister had a baby. I was thrilled for her. She lived 400 miles away, more than half-way to Sydney, and I took the children with me when I drove down to help her. Four days after we arrived, Max walked through the door of my sister's house and startled me with the news that we were returning to Sydney. So certain was he that this was for the best for us that he had put our collection of antique furniture in storage and boarded our horses with friends. He meant well: we were now in bad shape financially and he made the decision to move very quickly in the hope of finding a better situation in another place.

Having been raised in a financially secure home, I found poverty very hard to accept and I fought back tears as I tried to put a good face on this upheaval for the sake of my children. Starting over was difficult this time. Queensland was tropical, but we were returning to Sydney in winter. Our children did not have any warm clothing. I felt dreadfully embarrassed about taking them to a charity shop to buy second-hand wool sweaters. As usual, I hid my feelings from them, a game I learned to play well for years to come.

Money was scarce and we were unable to pay our storage bill, so the lovely antique furniture we'd collected was auctioned off. At least the storage company had the decency to send me our family albums.

I gave riding lessons to help pay for new furniture and hoped we would stay put long enough for the children to get through school. But further years of moving and hard times lay ahead.

In 1979, I was diagnosed with a tumour in the uterus; arrangements were made to admit me to the hospital for surgery. I had to wait four days before being admitted, and I thought of my mother's fate. My mind whirred as I lay in bed the night I had been diagnosed. 'What if I die? What if I don't live to see my children grow up?' When pessimistic thoughts came in, I desperately tried to put them aside. I could not let them get the better of me.

Suddenly some powerful force in my instinctual being seemed to take over and brushed the negativity from my mind. My thoughts became strongly positive, giving me directions to heal the tumour. How I got this information I do not fully know to this day. It wasn't a visual image or a voice in my head. I simply knew that I should bring white light into my third eye region near the centre of my forehead, then direct it as a ray through my body where the tumour was located to zap it.

In *The Third Eye*, the book I had read years before, T. Lobsang Rampa had talked extensively about this highly electrical body part. I could feel that area of my forehead pulsating as I attempted to hold on to the light, which I intuitively knew was energy. The energy kept floating away. I struggled desperately to focus as hard as I could to hold enough energy in that area. By now, readers, you have some idea of my work. At the time of writing, neither I nor anyone else has been able to find another person who can, with no hands on, heal and see inside the human energy field and body, also communicating with the body parts. So at this stage I can only tell you how I started and hope that if you want to heal others, your abilities will develop as mine did.

When I felt my forehead was full of energetic light, I then directed it as a fine ray through my body to the tumour. Once there, I concentrated to surge the energy ray through it. I had never in my life concentrated so hard on anything. My own will-power was the force behind my action but I believed that the energy itself was God.

I went through this process for two nights, but on the third night I could not do it successfully. It was as though I didn't have the power. At first I was disappointed because I realized I was healing myself with this mysterious technique. Then my mind said, 'It's okay! The tumour has gone.'

I put my hand on my abdomen in the area of the tumour and sure enough, it felt different and was no longer sensitive.

I kept my appointment at the hospital and when the doctor examined me, the puzzled expression on his face told me the tumour had disappeared. 'You won't find it because I healed it myself and it's gone, I zapped it with energy,' I said boldly. I learned very quickly that you don't talk to medical doctors that way. He doubted the truth of my words, but because my tumour had disappeared, he sent me home with the advice to see him if it ever returned.

Now that I had incontrovertible proof that I could heal myself, I accepted the truth of it. I was excited that I had instinctively found a self-healing method. Looking back, that experience was to give me knowing confidence that all is possible. Little did I know then that just eighteen months later I would have nine years of healing to accomplish, mostly unconsciously, because, as the result of brain damage, I was too out of it to zap myself knowingly.

All along, as my paranormal abilities emerged, I sought proof before taking them too seriously. But healing myself of this tumour built my confidence. It meant a great deal to me to have faith in myself, for there was no one in my family or circle of friends with whom I could discuss my abilities. My friends appreciated my clairvoyance when I made good predictions for them, but they had no interest in spirituality or the world of the paranormal. It was as though I had to hide my abilities. I had learned to be very guarded as the result of my early experience with my father, who felt it his duty to 'snap me out of it' when he caught me meditating at the dinner table.

As my paranormal abilities developed, the artistic side of

my being surfaced. I felt more creative and designed unusual clothing, which I wore with colourful headscarves. Max didn't mind, but when my children were teenagers, they'd tease me because I didn't dress the way 'ordinary' mothers did.

I was excited that my sixth sense abilities were increasing but I was soon to learn to be gentle in my approach.

A friend took me to visit her friend who owned a century-old home. As we sat waiting for the owner to come into the sitting room, I tuned into the house with my usual enthusiasm. The smell of an old person came to me, followed by a vision of an old man in a wheelchair who had died there. I interpreted this as having occurred many years ago. When I was introduced to the woman who owned the house, I asked her whether she knew the history of the place, and when she said no, I said, 'An old man in a wheelchair died in this room.'

She went white. 'That was my father, who passed away two years ago,' she answered, very shaken. I regretted my unbidden incursion into her space and tried to be more tactful from then on.

Psychic abilities are so natural to me that I expected others to have the same abilities. It was a good lesson for me to realize that many people are terrified of the intangible. I've learned to tread lightly, entering a person's energy field and body only when invited.

In time, my ability to read people and places psychically were to become a very important aspect of my healing work.

The sixth sense is a truly wonderful part of our system that has been de-empowered over the centuries from fear of the unknown. Isn't it true that humans fear anything that is not tangible or without matter? A perfect example is when children are caught staring into space, as the saying goes. They are very quickly brought back to planet Earth by teachers and parents, as I was by my father. This beautiful space is fifth-dimension level, far higher than our three-dimensional planet. It's God's territory. It's a safety zone to nurture and heal. People who truly meditate go there, where no earthly problem matters and time means nothing. I say truly because one has to transcend the fourth negative dimension but some hang in this, believing they are meditating. Young children go there easily, as they are still electrically connected to the fifth, not yet grounded in the earthly dimensions. I speak of true meditation later in this book.

Without fine tuning into my sixth sense, I certainly would not have accomplished the successful healings I have to my credit. I use the sixth sense to see inside energy fields and bodies for my work. It has actually developed to a point where I am able to communicate with body parts. I can travel from my abode to the far side of the world and work on body parts when they need attention. All this is done from the developed sixth sense, our intuition.

If you want to heal others, as I do, exercise this part of your brain. When the phone rings, try to guess who it is. You will be surprised once you remove the mental block and fear from your system. Don't forget to acknowledge yourself when you are correct with feelings of excitement or joy.

Another exercise you can use is to make yourself a pack of cards, six in all: two with a circle, two with a cross and two with a minus mark. See how many times you can guess the mark without looking at the card. Practise reading people's rings or bracelets. From these, you can pick up the owner's frequencies. Your intent must always be pure. Don't use these techniques to seek out negative information; always look to be positive. In other words, you are reaching for the highest levels of vibration.

Chapter 5

Divorce

Three years after we moved back to Sydney, we were able to make a down payment on land where we would build a house. To save money we again decided to live in a trailer while work on our new home progressed. I had the knack of teaming horses and riders to become successful in the show ring and had developed a lucrative business buying and training horses. My services were always in demand.

Within fourteen months we moved into our house. I was very happy, believing that Max would be less troubled and unpredictable now that we were back on our feet financially and settled in our own place. It was January 1981.

My happiness lasted all of three weeks. To my delight Max suggested we had dinner at a good local restaurant to celebrate our new home. Jane and Aaron went to spend the night with friends and we planned to drop Sarah at another friend's house on the way to the restaurant. I waited for Max to come home from work feeling glamorous in the outfit I had made for the occasion. When he did not arrive at the appointed time, my inner alarm went off. I feared that he might be on the town with the lads somewhere. How could he do this now we were on our way again? We lived in a new development where phones had not yet been installed so he could not call even if he wanted to. Perhaps he had a legitimate business reason to be late; perhaps he had had an accident. I worried and paced up and down.

Two hours later he pulled in. His mood was glowering and I feared the worst. The scene that followed defies description. Sarah tried to calm him down but Max took no notice. He went into the bedroom and fell into a deep sleep. In our distressed state, Sarah and I drove to friends and when we returned the following day, Max denied that he had upset us. His usual way of coping with these scenes.

Five days later I accepted an invitation for a girls' night out and I met four friends at a local inn. After dinner I felt ready to go home, but the others wanted to go on to another place thirty minutes away. My car was the only one large enough for all of us to fit in but I was still in a very emotional state so I told them no, I did not want to drive nor to go with them. My friend Pru was persuasive and volunteered to drive my car. The others chimed in with their encouragement and I gave in. By the time I got out to the car, I found I had to sit in the back. 'Great, it's my car and I'm thrown in the back seat,' I laughed.

Five minutes later, Pru overtook two cars on the highway and instead of straightening back into the driving lane, the car left the road, careered across a paddock, jumped a creek and went nose first into the opposite bank. I was knocked unconscious and can only relate the story as told by others.

The driver in front stopped to help. Our car was on fire and in danger of exploding so two men threw earth on the flames while others struggled to get us out. They left me in the car because they could find no pulse; my head was twisted in such a way that they thought that my neck was broken and I was dead.

Paramedics arrived thirty minutes later and discovered that I was still alive. They took us to a nearby hospital where two of us were admitted. My friend Helen had a broken pelvis and jaw. I had severe head injuries, a broken left arm and collarbone and my right foot was almost severed. Three years later, I was to discover from X-rays that my spine had been fractured in two or three places, but they missed that at the hospital.

I drifted in and out of consciousness for many days. Because of brain damage, I had no idea of my problems. I do remember having double vision and slurred speech. Visitors came and went but I had no idea who they were.

My broken arm became so badly infected that the plaster cast had to be removed. I felt numb all over, though numbness did not dull the excruciating pain in my spine. I could do nothing but lie on my back. I don't recall complaining of pain during my three weeks in the hospital, but I do remember fighting to be released. Finally, the doctors agreed to allow me home if I promised to have nursing care daily. I had more than 200 stitches to be tended and my broken arm needed exercising. My right foot was far from mended and a huge ulcer on my ankle verged upon the gangrenous.

My sister and my father lived hours away so I had very little support. Our acreage was far from busy urban life and we still had no phone. My daughter Jane was my wonderful mainstay. Max didn't seem able to accept the extent of my injuries: friends informed me years later that he thought I was just a bit bruised.

The first positive thought I had several weeks later was

that I had to leave Max. I would get well and divorce him. The plan gave me a certain amount of energy, but it would be eighteen months before I was capable of acting on it. In the beginning, I made trips to doctors whom I found to be of no help at all. Perhaps I was no help to them either. My head and speech were so befuddled I could not explain how I felt. Every morning, I prayed to open my eyes and not see two roof beams overhead where I knew there was just one. With my slurred speech, I was calling people I knew well by incorrect names. Short sentences planned in my head would come garbled from my mouth. Mentally I was terribly confused.

I stopped taking the prescribed medication. Doctors were very eager to give me neurology tablets, such as Valium. Thank God, I didn't succumb. I certainly remember having feelings of deep frustration and aggression which I know are emotions typical of neurological breakdown. The ulcerated wound on my ankle was so deep that the bone showed. I would expose my ankle to the sun, then fill the hole with calendula ointment made from marigold flowers. This worked so well that I was able to avoid the skin grafts doctors wanted me to have.

Months later, I found a doctor who treated football players and who had experience with head injuries. He told me that my brain was swollen and my condition would not improve until the cerebrospinal fluids in my head drained and returned to normal levels. As the brain is the slowest part of the human body to heal, it would take time. At last I had a doctor who helped me to understand what was happening. I could not wait for my next visit.

The condition of my head terrified me. The well-balanced person I'd always considered myself to be was gone. It had been replaced with an aggressive, frustrated creature with double vision and slurred speech who made little sense. It seemed everything had been taken from me. I was a physical and mental nothing.

When I could walk again, because of my double vision I had no idea what lay in front of me, flat ground or a rut. I had to summon courage from deep within to keep moving forwards without worrying about falling. 'Just keep forging ahead,' I would say to myself. Even when my thoughts were clear, I had trouble trying to converse. It was as though a switch in my brain was broken.

If I had been told then that I would need nine years of healing before total wellness was restored, I don't know how I would have reacted. Would I have given up, I wonder.

My relationship with Max was more strained than ever. We started selling our beautiful horses because it would be a long time before I could ride well enough to resume training them.

One day rolled into the next. I had never been so inactive in my life. I longed for my next visit to the football doctor, believing he could at least give me enough information to help me heal myself. On the day of my appointment his receptionist confronted me with the unpaid bill and said the doctor could not see me. I left, my face burning with shame. I had assumed that the fees had been paid on my behalf.

I decided that day that I would not have anything more to do with doctors and resolved to go it alone. A nurse friend told me that new brain cells could be educated to replace the damaged ones. This was very useful information. I made a vow to myself: 'If you have to re-educate your brain, you will make it better than before.'

Approximately nine months after the accident, my arm had straightened and I could use it again, and though still painful, my ankle wound was nearly covered with skin. But the left side of my body was numb, as were the soles of both my feet. My sentences still came out the wrong way round. I could remember things from the past but had little short-term memory, if any. And all my senses had diminished.

During the early years of my healing journey, I was definitely on automatic healing. My head wounds prevented any conscious effort to send directed energy rays. Maybe that's why it took so long. Looking back, it seems that once I decided to heal myself with God's help, the life-force took over. Every waking hour was spent tending wounds. My day would start with a prayer to remove my double vision the moment I opened my eyes, yet there it remained, year after year. But the depth of body memory kicked in: I practised trying to get short sentences to come from my mouth in running order and for the words to be clear and unblurred. It was several years before my limp disappeared. There is no doubt that having injuries embarrassed me but they also spurred me on to be normal again.

I was frustrated, often uncharacteristically angry and aggressive, common traits in persons with neurological damage. It was increasingly difficult to stay in the light to be positive, with the mounting pressures of rearing and schooling three children. I would literally force myself to reprogramme negative thoughts and feelings into positive ones. Flowers and the beauty of them worked for me. The memory of my success in healing my 1979 tumour remained and inspired me.

I intuited that to heal my brain, I had to move slowly in order to coordinate my movements with the speed of my brain activity. Although I was walking better, I had to remind myself constantly to slow down to what seemed like a turtle pace compared with my former speed. I worked on my speech all the time, keeping sentences short and forming them in my mind before I spoke.

As part of what I believe to be the Divine Plan of my healing experience, a special horse came into my life. My son Aaron had never really been interested in riding, but now he decided that he wanted his own horse. A friend found a gentle gelding named Fred, the sort of horse known in the Australian riding world as a 'bomb-proof paddock basher', a horse who didn't have a mean bone in his body. Predictably, Aaron's enthusiasm for riding lasted only three weeks, so I started riding Fred.

I would not be the well person I am today if it were not for that animal. Every day I'd haul myself aboard, no longer the polished show rider but a crouched bundle hanging on to the reins and saddle for dear life. Because of my double vision, it was entirely up to Fred to pick his way around the paddock. At a time when I was incapable of directing a spoonful of sugar into a mug without spilling it, riding helped re-establish my sense of rhythm and coordination. Although I did not realize it then, the bouncing movement of riding also helped to drain the excess fluid impairing my brain.

Twelve months' separation between couples is legally required in Australia before divorce becomes final. It had taken me eighteen months to obtain enough strength to get this far. Even though I was still desperately unwell, I wanted Max out of my life and I had felt overwhelming relief when he walked out the door. Divorce became final in 1983. After that it was hard to get him to keep up with the financial support he was legally obliged to give us.

It was crucial for me to keep my mind positive but I had to use precious energy to fight off negative feelings towards Max. One by one, our beloved horses had to be sold. Sarah had a lovely pony worth thousands of dollars because she had won many championships with him, but eventually even he had to be sold to bring our mortgage payments up to date. She was heartbroken and so was I. Several months later the mortgage fell behind again, so the property was repossessed anyway.

Losing the house was dreadful. I was able to obtain an advance from the insurance company on the settlement due to me from the accident and moved with the children to a lovely rented house – the thirtieth home I'd had since my marriage.

After my accident someone had put me in touch with an attorney who handled insurance cases. This man appeared to see a great opportunity to take advantage of a sick woman. I was entitled to a substantial settlement from the accident and desperately needed the money, but the lawyer dragged his feet for years. I wondered why, but couldn't get an answer. I intuitively knew that he was bad news. After five years of being put off, I discovered that I could energetically transport myself into his office. I could see him at his desk holding the phone. I don't know who was on the other end of the line, but the legal eagle was talking about delaying my case. Could the insurance company be paying him to keep me away from court?

I went to his office in person and told him I was turning

the case over to another attorney, but he demanded 5,000 dollars for my files. Without money I couldn't pay him.

I found another lawyer who had evidence that my first lawyer sometimes sided with insurance companies to the detriment of his own clients. He had enough information to force him to turn over my file.

I told no one of my ability to transport myself psychically into the attorney's office. In the future, I would use the same process to heal my clients from a distance. Spiritual powers are subject to strict universal laws that must be adhered to. I was allowed to use clairvoyance to help me escape the attorney's grasp, but I knew that to abide by the higher rules, I must not use this ability to invade others' lives. Having evolved to this level of transporting energy, one uses the ability with pure intent only. When I transport myself to work on body parts from afar, I go directly to that part, not invading any other aspect of the client's life. Anything else they are doing at that moment in time is none of my business. My only concern is to heal.

A common assumption is that it must be great fun to be in a restaurant, for example, and be able to see inside people.

'I wouldn't do such a thing,' I reply. My work begins only when I am approached for help.

At some level of consciousness, my psychic centres were being greatly developed during my own healing process though the ongoing struggle for daily existence took most of my attention. I often found myself in dark valleys of despair that I struggled to fight my way out of. During the latter stages of healing process, I felt I had gone too far into darkness and that the light at the end of the tunnel was out of my reach. I'd always been able to pull myself up before, no matter what happened, but now I feared I'd never be the bright, sunny person I'd been. As always, however, I fought these negative thoughts.

My children helped me to stay positive. They were helpful to me and managed to do really well at school. I was so proud of them. Friends today find it hard to believe that all of them are so positive and successful considering what they went through.

I didn't want to lean too heavily on my children so I sought spiritual help to end my gloom. A friend suggested that I see Denise, a clairvoyant with a lovely spiritual approach. In her readings, done only with a deck of playing cards, she felt that I was nearly at the end of the tunnel. 'You have almost reached the light,' she said. I cried with relief. Denise was like an angel — a 'ground angel' sent to help me along my earthly path. Ground angels can direct others through bleak or hazardous times. There have been so many of them on my journey that I have lost count.

Denise told me I had a spiritual guide who would make himself known. I had never heard of guides and was reluctant to show my lack of spiritual knowledge, so I didn't ask her what she meant. A friend confirmed that such guides give support to those in need.

Months later, a male voice with a French accent started coming into my head, introducing himself as Racob. As always, I approached this new occurrence cautiously. Was I hearing voices in my head because of my injuries? Was this just my overactive imagination at work? Since suffering brain damage in the accident, I felt I had to be more sceptical of these things than before.

Racob turned out to be a true guide for me, and I'll

always consider him as one of my most beautiful spiritual experiences. He informed me that he had died of measles in France in the eighteenth century at the age of twenty-four. He watched over my children wherever they went and told me of their every movement. He proved constantly that he knew where they were and what they were doing. I would say to the children, 'You had better behave or Racob will tell me.'

It certainly kept them in line. Once the girls were with friends at a horse show where they all developed a crush on the same young boy. Arrangements had been made for them to call me on our newly connected telephone and I was getting very concerned when one hour after the designated time I had heard nothing from them. Racob told me, 'Do not worry, Robyn, they will call.' They had been arguing jealously over the 'pony boy' as Racob called him. When they rang they were astounded that I knew about him. This incident, and many other such occasions, certainly proved Racob's existence.

One morning after Racob had been helping me for four years, I awoke to hear his voice calling me. He told me that he would be leaving me to help someone else. He assured me that my life was on the upsurge and I did not need him any more. I was distraught as I wondered how I would cope without him. It was three months, however, before Racob gently phased me out – I had feared he would be gone the following day.

By this time I was indeed functioning better and trying to rejoin the world. I started to drive again, working hard to follow the true line on the road rather than the one created by my double vision. I even resumed sewing to earn money, mustering all my concentration to sew a straight seam. I can't begin to describe the effort it took to relearn these simple tasks. God must have wanted me to rediscover my powers of concentration. Today, I use this powerful focus to direct energy when I heal others. I have learned to transport energy thousands of miles through telephone lines and now conduct several such sessions a day – not without cost to my own energy levels.

Chapter 6

The Revelation

I thought my healing would accelerate if I joined a meditation group. When the leader brought us out after half an hour I was amazed because it felt like five minutes. Apparently time as we know it means very little. Being in the meditative state did help my healing and provided an escape from earthly reality.

I discussed paranormal experiences with the women in the group, but discovered that no one questioned this side of life as much as I did, and I was not willing to rely on personal experiences in the realm of the unknown unless they were confirmed by hard day-to-day facts and actions.

After the group meeting one evening, I stopped for petrol on the way home. A woman named Tina pumped it and I could see and feel that she was very upset. She told me that she'd had a call that day from London telling her that her mother had died. I offered her my sincere condolences but by the time I arrived home I had all but forgotten our conversation.

As I lay waiting for sleep that night a woman's voice came into my head. Her English accent was hard to understand but though she did not actually say she was

Tina's mother, I knew she was. The woman gave me three messages about her last will — one for Tina, two others for her brother and sister. The messages meant absolutely nothing to me.

The following day, I was faced with the decision of whether or not to tell Tina. I did not want to upset her, nor did I want her to question my sanity, but my urge to tell her was strong. I have noticed that if it's right, the urge is powerful. This goes for general direction in your life: only go forward with your plans if it feels correct. Don't try to make them happen. After the seeds are sown, let them go, drop the wishes and desires. If the seeds are strong, they will take root at the right moment. If nothing much is happening in your life, take advantage of these rest periods to build the energy needed for the blossoming time.

When I went back and relayed the messages, Tina burst into tears and hugged me. She was enormously relieved to receive the information I brought her from her mother, the only person who could possibly have sent it. I now had proof that I could communicate with the dead. Channelling, the common name for this ability, became another part of my connection with the levels of vibration I now work with.

My cousin Meg came to stay with me from overseas and we decided to visit my brother, whom I hadn't seen for years. Dennis was confined to a wheelchair and was losing his sight but he obviously appreciated the little cakes we brought. He did not say a word to me, which I took as his way of showing his enduring anger for being institutional-ized. The staff told me that he sometimes spoke to them. Meg and I went back several times and it always took me days to recover from the sadness and guilt.

After Meg left, I went back many times. My children did not want to come, but Sarah did accompany me once and handled the experience of seeing her uncle very well. My father had married again and was living a long way from Sydney. If he knew of my visits to Dennis, he never mentioned them.

It was now 1986. I thought about spirituality and the paranormal constantly. I decided I wanted to read people's auras.

I knew that somehow a person's aura could be tapped into during a clairvoyant's reading. We now use the updated term *human energy field* to replace the word *aura*. Both relate to our electrical system. All the messages of past, present and future are there. I intuited this, that's why props such as cards, jewellery or keys, to tune into those programmes, did not interest me. I wanted to be the mouse searching for the data in the computer. But I had to start somewhere. I would ask my friends to pick a flower from my garden and clasp it gently in their hands. The purity of a flower appealed to me. However, even then, I knew it to be only a knob to turn the radio on, so to speak. My knowledge now tells me that the person holding the flower has placed their vibrational range upon it. I was able to pick up their vibration and thus enter their electrical system. I knew during the ensuing months that I was heading some-where on this spiritual journey but never did I truly think that I was to be a healer.

During this development period, the word *purity* kept entering my thoughts. Even though I needed money desperately, I would not accept payment for any spiritual services. Practising with my flower technique had strength-ened my clairvoyance. Now I asked God for the ability to read from personal contact only, using no props. This was to take some time. A friend arranged for me to appear on national television, demonstrating my flower-reading. From this appearance came an invitation to appear at Sydney's first three-day psychic fair. Even though weaknesses from my injuries still plagued me, especially when I was tired, I was excited at the opportunity.

My speech had improved: I now faltered only occasionally. My memory remained poor, so I still had problems with names and I had lost a lot of confidence. Driving into the city was my major concern because of my double vision. Although this was not so bad now, I had to drive with my head tilted back for clarity of sight and the drive was ninety minutes. The week before I had lost my car for a day in a car park lot and had to wait for all the other cars to clear before I could find it. Embarrassment and pride stopped me from reaching out for help on these occasions.

I pushed my worries aside and took off for my first day at the psychic fair on the proverbial wing and a prayer. I bought bouquets of flowers at a roadside stall on the way. There were many psychic readers at the fair and we were directed to give each client a fifteen-minute reading. On that first day, my readings were mostly about the person's house, job or relationship. I noticed that my clients were slow to leave the chair after the readings. They seemed to be quite dazed. I advised them to move slowly for thirty minutes to allow it to wear off, not knowing what 'it' was. I knew nothing about altered states then.

Towards the end of that first day I started to receive information about my clients' health, such as vitamins needed for their body, diet and blood disorders, and even the medical treatment they required. The clairvoyant across the aisle told me that when I took the flower the person had been holding, I would cup it in my hands for a moment, then put it down and do the reading. I've always closed my eyes during readings so I did not realize I was doing this.

By the middle of the second day, I felt an overwhelming urge to place my hands above my head, fingertip to fingertip. Then I moved my arms down slowly and discovered that I could see inside the clients' bodies. I was seeing body parts and feeling their condition with what I can only describe as a deep knowing. This was fascinating and may have helped my clients, but fearing ridicule, I did not tell people that I was seeing inside them. People ask me if I was surprised: somehow I knew I could do it.

On the third day of the fair, I was introduced to Bert who held weekly healing evenings in his house. I liked him, and by a wonderful coincidence he lived close to my home, so I was able to attend his meetings for eight months.

On these group healing evenings we practised sending energy to hospitals and nursing homes, using concentrated effort to transport it. Bert encouraged us to approach spirituality as a science. He also encouraged us to start thinking of God as positive energy.

This troubled me. I had always envisioned God as a man, as I had been taught in church Sunday school. He lived in a magnificent garden filled with angels playing harps. This man knew everyone's actions and thoughts at any time all over the planet, especially if you were naughty or lied, and He would punish you if you deserved it. Nevertheless, the notion of God as *energy* was compelling.

During one of the evening healing meetings, a new member asked me to prove my abilities. I told him about how he had hurt his knee in a bicycle accident as a young boy and that he had a tiny scar behind his ankle bone as a result.

He replied that he didn't have a scar on his body but everyone urged him to take off his shoes and socks to look. I hoped I hadn't made a fool of myself, but the scar was exactly where I'd predicted it would be. This provided another boost to my confidence, which I needed badly.

It was not easy to change my concept of God in human form to one of God as energy and I was concerned that I would not be able to feel the same love. Now my love for God is even deeper. I also questioned whether humans are permitted to use energy in this way. Is it an allowable law of the universe? I always wanted to be a good person and this thought gnawed at me until I'd convinced myself that Bert must have been evil and I considered quitting the group. How narrow-minded I must have been then, and how wrong!

Healing myself was proceeding, but haltingly. Maybe I was moving too fast in developing skills for healing other people and neglecting myself. Anyway, those negative thoughts about Bert slowed my excursions into higher levels of vibration; perhaps they were meant to.

Although the urge to heal others was strong, I was not ready to go forward, yet amazingly, the incredible responsibility attached to the work never worried me. First I had to sort out questions about the depth of my love for God. I needed to develop faith in my powers before I was ready to tell the world I was a healer and I needed more confidence in my ability to handle life after the accident. I find that most people who suffer severe body or head trauma have their self-confidence shattered. Some never regain it. I had to fight every step of the way to recover what I'd lost.

I had very limited knowledge of the human body and needed to study anatomy. Although I could see body parts, I didn't know the names of organs and glands or how they worked together. I doubted my diagnostic ability and depressed myself by thinking that clients would have to show me a diagnosis from their doctor before I could heal them and that didn't make sense: if I was to be a healer, surely I should be able to diagnose a person's disease? With all these unanswered questions and problems to solve, I left the healing group and eight months of discovery and revelation behind.

Then I had a talk with God and laid out three positive things I needed:

1. If you want me to heal others, please let me know in a manner that will be too strong for me to ignore it.
2. I will need to be able to diagnose their problems correctly.
3. I would like to be able to heal as well as Jesus. Please.

Now I waited for my answer from God.

I used to walk along the banks of a river with my dog. One day we came upon a magnificent willow that had been a victim of debris washed down in a flood which had gouged a deep wound in its trunk. New growth was filling the gaping hole in the same way the hole in my ankle was now covered by new skin.

The willow stood strong and proud, a testament to the power of healing. The tree was just getting on with it, just doing it, not wanting anyone to feel sorry for it, certainly retaining its own dignity. That lone willow gave me strength to complete my own healing and to realize that I was still feeling like a victim because recovery had been so slow. I still had thoughts like, 'Oh God, what did I do wrong to deserve this agony?' even though I had come so far.

During healing we have to keep looking back to realize how far we've come. We somehow easily forget to do this in our eagerness to reach the light at the end of the tunnel. A lone willow tree snapped me out of feeling sorry for myself.

Only one of my horses remained, a gelding named Royalty, the thoroughbred I had bred to be my champion of champions. I had not been able to establish him yet because of my health. His physical conformation was near perfect, his movement poetry in motion. His nature was as sweet as a puppy dog's. He always looked forward to my daily visits and never failed to come galloping towards me, whinnying madly; we adored each other. However, I had no alternative but to sell Royalty he was worth enough money to get me through to the end of the year when I hoped the lawyer would manage to have a court date set for my hearing on the insurance case.

I had to lead Royalty into the buyer's trailer because he would not leave without me. I ran into the house, unable to stop sobbing, in total despair. When the tears stopped, I had a feeling that something was trying to break my spirit. I stood in my kitchen, pulled myself up to my full height, raised my arms toward the sky, and with clenched fists shouted, 'Okay, come on, come on, no matter what you throw at me I won't break. You will not break my spirit.' Overwhelming numbness followed.

Thirty minutes later a phone call came from my lawyer announcing that my hearing had been advanced and the case would be heard by the end of the year. Days later the owners of our rented house decided they wanted to move back in, but we found another in the same area, which meant that the children could stay at the same school. This would be move number thirty-one since I left my childhood home.

I was now into my fifth year of healing. My back still hurt constantly and though my eyes were stronger, I still suffered from double vision. By now insurance company doctors were examining me. One said cynically, 'Oh, you get back pain, do you?' His tone told me that he didn't believe me. He might as well have said, 'That's what they all say.' He ordered X-rays for me and I knew he was thinking to himself, 'We'll make sure you don't get any money for your back.'

The X-rays revealed two fractures, possibly three. Unfortunately I missed seeing the doctor's face when he received the results. To this day, I don't know why these fractures weren't discovered and treated earlier.

I still had trouble with tests set by neurologists; my brain still wasn't normal. But the doctors were amazed that my speech was so clear considering the severity of my head injuries. 'Which speech therapy clinic have you been attending?' they asked and were surprised when I told them I had worked on it myself. Although my speech was becoming clear, if I asked too much of my brain, it would sometimes shut down. It was as if someone had pulled a blind down in front of it. All would become black and blank. These embarrassing moments could occur at any time. I had become very adept at disguising my abnormalities.

Apart from trying to heal, I had great stresses to contend with, nearly always financial. I wanted to give my children so much and felt guilty for what had happened to our family. They were in high school now and their education was important. I wanted them to have the university education I had missed.

Aaron had been selected as an exchange student to go to the USA. I was proud of him but my heart ached when I said goodbye at the airport knowing I would not see him for a year. I was able to obtain a small loan from the bank, enabling him to travel, because my hearing date was only months away.

Sarah had left for college to study communications. Thank God, Jane was still with me. Friends I'd made while showing horses disappeared now that I wasn't showing any more. I also found that several of my friends couldn't handle my illness. I was incredibly lonely.

However, my relationship with God was developing. I had framed a lovely poem that told how God carries you when you are in trouble. I was still thinking of God in human form and could see myself sitting in the lap of a giant man, my head against His chest. This father-figure made me feel safe. I had totally surrendered to God when I was still quite sick. I'd cried out from my bed, 'God, I don't seem to be making a good job of my life. I think you would do a better job of it.' Now I felt that I was given comfort and help every day.

At last, the long-awaited court hearing came and I endured three harrowing days of it. Emotions I had buried during the physical healing process surfaced: fear, apprehension, dread. There was no need to be afraid; with the injuries I'd received in the accident, my case was strong. A list of them covered three foolscap pages, starting with severe brain damage, loss of speech, memory and concentration, double vision, hearing disability – and that was only in my head. Then there were my three spinal fractures and all the other ones. Nevertheless, I played the drama queen and threw myself on the mercy of the court to obtain maximum compensation allowable in the Australian justice system. I did receive a large amount: a quarter of a million dollars.

In time my performance bothered me and I felt unworthy of the money. I did not like the Robyn I had been in court, feeling as if I had betrayed myself and God. Year by year as I grew stronger, my guilt increased for receiving compensation for conditions the doctors and judge believed would last for the rest of my life.

My conscience started overwhelming me and I felt that my insurance award was tainted money. I had to let it go, and did so by giving away large sums and making bad investments. I now realize that my healing power would never reach the perfection I aspire to had I kept the money. It would have blocked my progress.

Money can and does stand in the way of real happiness. I truly believe wealthy people can only be happy by sharing their wealth and supporting worthwhile causes. I won't work with clients who are awaiting compensation for body injuries. They will nearly always hang on to the ailments to receive the money.

Chapter 7

Seeking Perfection

Aaron and Sarah were away at school and Jane was rooming with friends. It was 1989 and for the first time in my life I was free to strike out on my own. I had plenty of money now and decided to use it to try to build up a fashion design business. I had a passion for beautiful clothing and believed my investment in myself would pay off. My *nothing is impossible* mode took over.

The lone divorcee took off to the Philippines where I could manufacture beautiful clothing at low cost because labour was plentiful and cheap. I had no business plan, just a desire to find factory space and get started. I was still not well, but that did not worry me much. The hardest part was missing my children. And my intuitive strength to heal others was not of the strength I had asked for in my affirmations to God. I now realize that I had to become totally strong, both physically and mentally, for the journey that lay ahead.

I rented a large apartment in Manila, employed a maid who had very little English, purchased a car and hired a driver named Jimmy. When I look back at that period of my life, I doubt very much that I was functioning properly.

Now I realize that my neurology system was not 'on the pace'. My brain would still shut down if overtaxed, even though my speech was better and the double vision slowly but surely corrected – it would now only occur in the evening when I was tired. My back still hurt. I joined an aerobics group and, for the first time since my accident, I was physically working out again. It felt good.

The government of the Philippines was unstable and rival forces were attempting to overthrow the president, Ferdinand Marcos. I was walking into a perilous situation but my naiveté seemed to protect me. My apartment building was also home to United Nations representatives from England who were involved in major road building in Manila. During one of the coup attempts, we were interned in our complex by a squadron of armed guards because of the danger from attacks on the army camp a few miles away. One afternoon when we were locked in, we were gathered at my place when two planes started shooting rockets at each other. We sipped gin and tonic and gazed at them through sliding-glass doors as if we were watching a giant television screen. Towers of thick smoke rose from the streets. We heard nearby gunfire. It seemed surreal to be socializing while people were dying out there.

The carnage in Manila was everywhere. Driving me to a meeting one day, Jimmy went along the oceanfront on a wide boulevard lined with tall palms silhouetted against a ravishing pink sky. I was enjoying the moment when he suddenly pointed to three bodies with their throats cut slumped against the sea wall. I had to struggle against nausea. The atmosphere of unrest distressed me. I was seeing the seamy side of life and how cheap life could be. Why had I come to this place, I asked myself.

Added to the distress of political unrest was my frustration at not finding suitable factory space for the quality garments that I wanted to market. The places I looked at were dark and dingy, nothing like the bright, happy workshops I had in mind. Finally I gave up the idea of finding anywhere, hired seamstresses and set up a workroom in my apartment. My friends called it my penthouse cottage industry. Before long, I had twenty perfect silk suits and dresses.

My plan was to take these samples to existing workshops to be copied exactly at a decent price. I ordered a shiny chrome rack to hang my beautiful garments on. The woman who delivered it asked me to take her back to her shop. Jimmy and I obliged and on the way, she asked me many questions about the distinctive-looking car. I thought she was just making conversation but, looking back, I feel she had something else in mind.

The following week she called to say she had friends exporting clothing to Hawaii. Would I like to meet them? My heart soared and my mind revved up at the idea of breaking into a market that would be a wedge into the USA. I thought I had it made.

Jimmy drove me to the address on the other side of Manila. It was a wealthy area where high walls with large steel gates surrounded all the homes. As I stood in front of the 10-foot-high gate with my garments over my arm, I was overwhelmed with terror. I wanted to run, but I talked myself out of it. Still, I knew I should be careful about showing my samples to strangers. They might steal my designs and copy them. It happens all the time in the garment industry. I had Jimmy put the dresses back in the car.

After twenty minutes inside I felt comfortable enough to send a maid for my samples. A minute later, three maids came screaming into the room saying, 'Ma'am, your car has been taken by three men with guns. They have taken your driver. They will kill him.' I reeled with fear. In these raids the driver was indeed usually shot. Then Jimmy staggered through the door reporting that the thieves had driven him around the block and thrown him out of the car. His bright shirt was shredded and he was bleeding from a head wound. Why didn't I heed my sixth sense? Because all I could think of was a USA market. Now, I told myself, you have lost your car and put your driver's life in jeopardy. Chastened, I thank God to this day that the thieves did not kill Jimmy. I had put materialism and success above all else. In my haste to make huge sales and money I had not heeded my sixth sense.

We took a cab to the police station, a filthy place, to report the incident. As I was shown into a large room to speak with the head of the car-theft division we walked past tiny cells where unkempt humans were caged like animals.

After I had dealt with the paperwork, reality set in and for the first time I had the shakes inside as well as outside. My car and the precious samples that represented a year's work were gone. Tearful and unsteady, I was accompanied to my apartment. An officer wanted to be sure I was all right.

All I wanted to do was fly home to Australia but I could not leave right away because I had an army of workers depending on my paycheques. There were no unemployment benefits in the Philippines and I could not desert the staff until I'd found them other work. It was three weeks before I could leave with a clear conscience.

When I arrived home I rented an apartment on the beach thirty minutes south of Sydney in my home town of Cronulla, where I felt safe and secure. I wondered whether my car would ever turn up, but I had little hope of it. The police had told me that stolen vehicles were usually taken to country areas and stripped. I had visions of tribal people, deep in the tropical forest, wearing my line of executive silk clothing. No one believed I would ever receive payment from the insurance company in the Philippines. It took me straight back to old feelings of hating the world, wondering if anything would ever go right for me. Unreasonably, I blamed God for my bad luck. However, my natural space was beautiful, my view of the ocean superb. Again, I drew on nature to heal.

I started jogging along the shoreline, surprising myself with my strength. This was proof that my body was flowing again. It was exhilarating to feel physically whole and I entered several marathons – I had been working out daily in Manila. At times it felt as if I was in training for more than a marathon – I was in training for the rest of my life. I now realize that becoming so physically fit helped me climb to higher levels of vibration that were still needed for my work ahead. Sometimes I felt I could soar through the air and join the bright white light where the ocean meets the sea on the horizon at Cronulla. Good and fulfilling feelings for God returned; it was becoming a one-to-one relationship. Finally, I didn't have to be carried: I was running hand in hand with God.

Twelve months later I went back to Manila to collect a small insurance payment for my car. My love of clothing and determination to be successful spurred me on to resume my business. Don't be a wimp, I said to myself.

This time, I found the exact factory I needed to produce quality clothing. I obtained orders from boutiques in Sydney from my samples and went to Manila on short trips to oversee manufacture, staying in safe hotels. I met international embassy people and my social life picked up. I was invited to wonderful parties, which was great fun as I love music and dancing. They were restrained affairs with no drugs and little alcohol. My renewed connection to the spirit gave me a sense of protection and I went to places that were considered dangerous, such as the huge fabric market, with large sums of cash to buy my materials.

Poverty was pervasive and I found it hard not to give money to beggars although the locals don't encourage foreigners to do so. Women would take their babies into the streets in cardboard boxes while they sold cigarettes one at a time to get money for food. It was heartbreaking. Though I could not help every needy person, I supported an orphanage and often went there to help with the babies. The handful of nuns at the orphanage cared for them devotedly and I was deeply moved when I was made an honorary Sister of Mercy by the Catholic nuns of Manila.

My orphanage work allowed me freedom of conscience to enjoy the positive aspects of the beauty of the flowers and palm trees along the road instead of dwelling on babies in boxes on the kerb. I was always trying to convert the negative to the positive in my mind. I now realize that my time in the Philippines was more than a business venture; it was integral for spiritual growth and preparation for what lay ahead.

I had heard stories of a fifteenth-century church in Baclaran on the outskirts of Manila where all prayers were answered. The church had a waiting list of two years for their special prayer meetings. I had to go there. The huge stone church was packed. Entering through a side door, I was shocked to see a procession of worshippers moving down the aisle on their knees, fingering their rosary beads, muttering their prayers with heads bowed. By the time they reached the altar, their knees were bleeding. I couldn't relate this mournful procession to spirituality and I wanted to scream, 'Get off your knees, you don't have to bleed to pray to God.' I left without knowing why their prayers were answered. I would understand much later.

When I had evolved to a higher level of spiritual communication, I saw that God doesn't speak any language and that successful communication is achieved by visualization and feeling – emotion. Prayers are more likely to be answered if you communicate your desire to God by visualizing, keeping it as simple as possible. Sow that seed of prayer with an emotion, for example, 'I will be so happy if it becomes true', or 'I will cry with joy'. Your concentrated effort must be totally focused in the now. The fortunate people who were given the opportunity to pray in Bacalaren church after such a long wait would have been entirely focused upon their prayer. This was a great moment and their emotions would have been intensified from the pain of crawling on their knees on stone. It would have been the boost in energy needed to reach the high vibrational level of God for their prayer to be answered.

Prayer is very intense, emotionally connected to our electrical field. Some may find the force of this communication with God hard to accept. They will really believe that our prayers have been answered from the spoken language. But there is no doubt in my mind that as they were praying these people would have been visualizing their need in their mind's eye. I believe that the pain that has influenced our spiritual growth in the past will diminish as we advance into a more enlightened, intelligent approach to life.

My social circle was growing to include people from many countries and all walks of life. This joyful group taught me to live and let live and not judge others. Trusting people has been a dicey area for me. My natural tendency is to love and trust everyone but I learned the hard way that some people are not to be trusted.

By 1992, the Australian economic recession hit the market for expensive women's clothes and I was badly affected. To keep going I came up with a range of tracksuits and jackets designed for members of football teams popular throughout the country. I also set up home-selling parties for clothing which I was buying and importing from Asia. These enterprises worked but fell far short of my financial goals. I had now found factories in the Philippines that could manufacture any kind of clothing well but my hopes of going into large-scale marketing were dampened by economic conditions. I was forced to sell my city apartment. I felt financially and emotionally drained.

I had worked hard to achieve perfection in my manufacturing but early on I discovered that quality control was lax in the Philippines. I became so frustrated with workers taking short cuts that I bought a magnifying glass 6 inches in diameter and insisted that every stitch be checked. One day I would be viewing the human body through a different magnifying glass of my own, seeking the same perfection.

I believe that the development of my business skills contributed later to my success as a healer. In the past I had impatiently dashed through life, just as the garment workers had sloppily raced through their work. Learning to take extra care and settle for nothing less than the best profoundly influenced my healing work. Mistakes cannot be risked with the human body.

During the autumn of 1992, the only way to obtain orders was to allow outlets to delay payment for up to six months. I was in no position to carry their debt and the future looked dark. At first I could laugh no matter how tough things looked, but now the battle had been so long and so hard that I had forgotten how to feel optimistic. I'd look at my lifeless eyes in the mirror and pray that God would turn the lights back on. Worst of all, I had no love in my life. The children were away. The men I'd dated didn't last, and most of my new friends had disappeared. I had no one to talk to, no one to care. The thought of not being able to feel love any more caused me to think seriously of ending my life.

Chapter 8

The Light Is Turned On

One sunny afternoon in Cronulla my friend Melissa came over. I went to fix tea and cookies, leaving her in the living room.

'My God, Robyn,' she called. 'There's a glow from your walls, like an aura or something. It's so beautiful.'

'I'm glad you can see it,' I replied. 'I've noticed it too but thought I was imagining that the white paint just looked brighter.'

'No, the walls are definitely glowing.'

Word spread to others who came to visit and absorb the wonder of it. Because I had worked hard to lift myself from my low vibrational period late in 1992, I assumed that the glowing walls were part of everything in my life looking brighter until Melissa and others verified that bright white light actually shone from my walls. I loved my glow; it made me feel vibrant. During the ensuing months its beam expanded to approximately 6 feet and it seemed to me that Divine energy was present in my apartment.

I felt proud of the work I had done to get rid of negative thoughts and feelings. Whenever I had sad thoughts about my past and those who had added to my pain, I'd steer myself to the mirror, stare into my eyes and tell myself I needed those experiences for spiritual growth. Accepting complete responsibility for the programme I'd given myself before entering this lifetime was important if I was to move beyond it.

We set the exam papers before we enter our lifetime: the older the soul, the more intense the exam. The ticks on the test paper are black, representing negative energy – the Devil – or white, representing the positive Divine energy. At the end of the life journey, if you use your imagination to see your energy field as the test paper, and the ticks as black or white frequencies, you want your test paper to be full of white or positive frequencies. It takes hard work for forgiveness and purity of mind to keep moving forward, with love energy surging in our hearts. The work is required to enable us to have enough power to return to the fifth or Divine dimension that we came from, bearing in mind that we need to thrust from the three earthly dimensions through the fourth, which is the negative. Negative thoughts and feelings, drug intake, abuse of alcohol and over dosage of chemical supplements will build black ticks. However, if we have built our energy field with good frequencies, not bad, there will be no problem in returning to Heaven. That's why I say, 'Imagine your field as your wings to Heaven.'

I'd driven myself out daily with clothing samples over my arm, treading the streets of Sydney looking for stores that would order and pay up-front, a hard task during a recession. Whenever I obtained an order, however small, my self-esteem soared.

I had been experiencing surges of energy radiating through my head so strongly that I was afraid I would drift off and away. This could occur at any time or place during waking hours and the rushes left me light-headed. I knew my neurology very well after contending with my head injuries and concluded that these strange bursts of energy were spiritual, not physical. I did not usually want to seek advice from a clairvoyant, feeling that every time I did so, I was disempowering myself and also challenging my trust in God. But finally, I decided to see Denise again. She was the psychic who had proved to be helpful in the past.

It felt good to see this special soul and I tried to describe my experiences. 'I'm having floating sensations, as though I'm lifting off the ground. It takes all of my self-control to hang on to the planet. I feel it's a manifestation of spiritual growth, but it's frightening.'

In her wise and centred way Denise said, 'You are right to assume that the experiences are spiritual. I'm not sure where you're headed but your vibrational level is the highest I've ever encountered. Visualize yourself hanging on to a tree trunk and pant short breaths the next time you feel yourself floating. This will keep you grounded.

Over the following year I had twelve more lifting episodes. I see this period of my journey as the merging of my earthly outer consciousness with my inner, spiritual being. The energy shift created by this was very powerful. I now believe that many people get to this point in their development but are not able to cope with the transition. Those who can handle this fine-tuning will come to know joy, peace, harmony and perfect love. The two consciousnesses have to merge, and together strive for the energy needed to keep connection to the highest vibrational level obtainable in our lifetime.

Soon I was directed to a Sydney ashram by another

ground angel who belonged to my tennis group. There I found a book, *The Mystery of the Mind*, by a powerful spiritual teacher, Swami Muktananda, which answered many of my questions. Though Muktananda had died a few years earlier, his words spoke directly to me:

> The mind is the mystery of human life. It can be the garden of joy or the secret path to death. It can show us heaven or it can take us to hell . . . the same mind that is the cause of suffering is also the means of attaining the highest happiness. One who has truly understood the mind and has brought it under his control lives in bliss. One who has made the mind pure, strong, and still is able to accomplish anything. The scriptures of India are almost entirely devoted to describing means of purifying and stilling the mind. . . . The scriptures and the saints say that the individual soul is not a separate entity but a part of God. It is completely pure and the embodiment of supreme bliss.

I was delighted to have my ideas about mind control so beautifully affirmed and amplified. During my short time with the ashram, I connected telepathically with Muktananda, who gave me strength to go forward. He was a wonderful influence and I loved him very much. However, ashram life was not for me. Daily services featured chanting in Sanskrit, which no one at the ashram could translate. I didn't like singing words I didn't understand so I left after a short time, silently thanking Muktananda for his wisdom. My feelings about India have now changed somewhat. I feel that for many reasons the level of consciousness has fallen.

By mid-year strange but wonderful things were happening. One day, my cousin Megan and I were driving home from Sydney to my apartment in Cronulla. The road curved along the bay. We saw the beautiful arc of a rainbow ahead and suddenly we were in it. Usually a rainbow is out of reach but there we were, driving through a shower of brilliant colour for ten minutes. Thank goodness Megan was with me to verify that it really was like that. Why is it we always feel the need of witnesses for what we consider to be phenomenal occurrences? During the following months, rainbows twice came right on to my balcony.

I could see the sky from my fifth-floor apartment while seated in my living room. On several nights I saw myself sitting in the curve of a crescent moon, as though it were a rocking-chair. By now I was accepting these marvellous things like a delighted child, though I lacked the confidence to tell anyone about them, especially after my neurological history. Still, the thought constantly popped into my head, 'Let the good times roll.'

The most extraordinary of these experiences occurred in November 1993 when I became involved in the case of two young naval pilots who had gone missing. The search for their plane was covered nightly on television. As I watched, I realized I was tuning energy into one of the pilots. I knew he was still alive, though badly injured. His friend was dead but he stayed with the body, hoping to be found. They had crashed in Australia's Blue Mountains, a rugged area with escarpments hundreds of feet deep.

I became fully engrossed, trying to send energy to keep the pilot alive. I was actually going through his pain and suffering, even to the point of smelling the stench of foxes in a cave where he had dragged his friend. The smell was so rank that he was dry-retching. When the air search was called off, his father turned to higher energies for help. The TV station I had appeared on several years earlier called me. By this time I was able to sketch a map of the place where the plane had crashed. I told the pilot's father he was still alive, but I knew from the weakening of the frequency that he was fading. I could not hold him. After I gave the rescue team the map, it took them thirty hours to reach the plane through the rugged terrain. By that time I had lost contact with the pilot. Both men were dead when the search party arrived. Nightmares of thrashing through the bush looking for him didn't cease until the full naval funeral brought closure for me.

I didn't know it at the time, but there's an ancient Native American belief that a person who accompanies another on their death journey will start a new life. Mine began a month after the pilot died. It started, strangely enough, with a wrong number and a person whose first name, like Racob's, began with R.

In December 1993, a man named Ron called me. He was looking for a friend whose last name was Welch. Ron told me that his friend was visiting his parents near me so he was calling every Welch in the phone book. He called back many times and we spoke and flirted for hours on the telephone. Then, out of the blue, he invited me for a two-week holiday in Kauai where he had rented a condo. When I learned it was in Hawaii and that the place had two bedrooms I became interested. Two clairvoyants had told me that I would marry a man with the initial 'R'. On my first trip to Denise, she had also predicted an overseas trip, which I would not be taking alone. 'You must go, don't change 'your mind,' she had said. Could Ron be the mysterious Mr R? He sent me a photo. He was a single professional man. I liked his voice. I said yes. It seemed totally right although my family were horrified to think I would take off with a man I had never met.

I had Christmas with them and met Ron the following day at the airport. I must admit that when I saw him, I knew he was not the one for me, but I also felt reassured that I would have no problem with him over my separate bedroom stipulation.

When we arrived in Kauai I thought I had landed in heaven. The north side of the island astonished me: it was gorgeous and lush beyond anything I'd ever seen and it engulfed me with positive energy that seemed to spring from the earth itself. The ground seemed almost holy, with grace pouring out to give a wonderful feeling of peace and serenity. Many people know that unexplainable spiritual events occur on Kauai, and I was soon to discover this for myself.

The apartment was lovely and close to the beach. On our first evening, I playfully tumbled in the aquamarine crystal waves and found myself swimming by the wharf used in the movie *South Pacific*. I couldn't believe how fast everything had happened. But it often does when energy decides it's time to create a shift. By the third day, I started to feel that I should stay in Kauai. I tried hard to push these feelings aside and thought how ridiculous I was. On the fourth day, Ron heard that his daughter had been injured in a road accident and flew home to Australia, leaving me to stay on in the apartment. Ron was another ground angel. He knew nothing of my healing talent: I felt he would have a cynical attitude towards it so reluctantly I did not offer to help his daughter.

By the fifth day, the urge to stay was even stronger despite my mixed feelings: my precious daughters were in Australia, yet my son was in San Francisco so I'd be closer to him if I stayed . . . I'd had talks in Sydney about selling my 1994 fashion line but had not signed contracts. I had worked hard to become a success in Australia, but now I thought about getting my clothing into the US market. My finances were drained, and the idea of being close to the mainland of the USA appealed. The pros and cons of staying churned through my mind but actually the urge to stay in Kauai was the strongest factor.

That afternoon I gazed at the mountains on the other side of Hanalei village. I saw them as a row of waves curved on top, standing vertically in all their glory. I silently told them, 'You are so beautiful.' With that, the mountains spiritually swept me up, holding me tenderly as they gave me their message: 'We love you, we will always be with you. Go on.'

It took me a long, long time to tell anyone of that experience, afraid that people would think me crazy. Things are different now and many people realize that we are electrically connected to everything on this planet. Everything has an energy field, even rock, and those who don't accept this do not bother me any more. My father used to say, 'What will the neighbours think if you're not a good girl?' I don't know a single one of those neighbours now. I don't ignore others' feelings but I do believe one should live one's own life according to one's conscience and have self-respect. Paradoxically my father also said, 'A person who loses their self-worth has lost everything,' and that seems very wise.

That night was New Year's Eve and I was invited to a

party in the magnificent Princeville Hotel. At the stroke of midnight, I took the hand of the elderly woman next to me to wish her 'Happy New Year, Happy 1994,' but what came out of my mouth was, 'Goodness, darling, you are having gall-bladder trouble.'

Her husband's eyebrows flew up. 'Is that why she is in such pain?' he asked. 'I wanted her to go to the hospital for a checkup, but she insisted on coming here tonight.'

'I can fix her,' I blurted.

I met with Alberta the following day and discovered that for a woman of almost seventy she was in remarkably good health, but the tissues of her bile duct had thickened and were blocking the flow of bile. Within four sessions I was able to stretch the ducts to create a stronger flow and her pain disappeared.

I thought back to 1987 when I had told God that I needed irrefutable evidence that I was destined to be a healer. Ability to diagnose illness was one of the three things I demanded. Now I was thrilled by my spontaneous diagnosis and rapid healing of Alberta, my first real client. But what didn't quite sink in was that I was now truly embarking upon my real journey through life.

Chapter 9

My Real Journey Begins

I would stay in Hawaii. My encounter with the spirit of the mountains had given me the support I needed. But how would I accomplish the move?

Flying to Australia and back would cost a lot and might weaken my resolve and I had to be positive in order to move forward. I decided to call my daughter Jane and ask her to pack up my apartment and organize a garage sale to clear all my possessions except a few precious things. I considered how I would explain all this: my move to Kauai was probably enough to convince the family that brain damage was causing me to drop out. If I told them I was becoming a healer, they'd be sure that I'd lost my reason. Finally I found the courage to call.

'Jane, darling, it's Mum! Yes, I'm wonderful, I wish I had words to describe this magnificent island. As a matter of fact, it's so beautiful here, I think I'll stay a while,' I blurted.

'What?' Jane shouted.

'Jane, if I come home to pack up my apartment, it will cost too much, so I wondered if you would do it for me and have a garage sale. Sarah will probably help you. I've never asked you girls to do anything for me. I can't explain my feelings at the moment. All I can say is the future has the answers.' Emotion overwhelmed me, I was calling into a silence, but Jane agreed to help before I was reduced to begging.

A short while later Sarah rang. 'Mother, what are you doing, for God's sake?'

Little did she realize that I was staying in Hawaii precisely for God's sake, but that was much too complicated to spell out.

'You are being totally irresponsible. Come home,' she demanded.

'No, Sarah, I have to stay. I can't explain now, I can only tell you the same thing I told Jane, the answer is in the future.' I felt very guilty about leaving my children and I wondered whether they would ever understand. Deep within, since my mother's death, I had felt totally responsible and focused on my family. Now here I was wanting to heal the world, which meant stepping outside my tribe for a time. I guessed they would feel pain, especially as they had no idea of my dream. Their feelings would be of total loss. Several years later, Jane told me that they cried as they packed up my apartment. 'Mum, it was as if you had died.'

It took a long time for my family to accept my new path and for years my visits home were contentious and unbearably sad. I discovered that my children did not believe their mother should leave the tribe although they no longer required attentive mothering. Their lack of enthusiasm for my healing journey was heartbreaking; if there was one positive side to their dismay it was that by working on the pain in my own heart I developed empathy and greater ability to heal other heartsick folk.

My two-week stay at the condo Ron paid for ended all too soon and I moved to an inexpensive hotel while I sought a permanent place I could afford. I read every ad in the newspapers and told shopkeepers that I was looking for a place. Then a ground angel called on the third day, just as I was losing hope, and recommended that I speak to Shirley Hall, who had a Tahitian-style hut on the beach that she might rent out.

My heart leapt. Please God, this rental has to work, I entreated. It was ten-thirty at night when I learned about the hut and I had to be out of the hotel the following day. Despite the late hour I called Shirley and the hut sounded wonderful. She picked me up the following morning to drive me there. The hut was right on a white sand beach surrounded by palm trees and bright tropical flowers. The shower was on the outside but enclosed by foliage and completely private. The place had an idyllic, timeless charm I found irresistible. Shirley rented it to me at a fair rate and I moved in.

In no time people who had heard of Alberta's gall-bladder healing called for appointments. The first three who came also had gall-bladder malfunction. It seemed that I was to learn my craft by having three or four people in a row with the same ailment. There is no doubt in my mind that I was guided during my time on Kauai.

I was invited to join certain spiritual communities but an inner voice told me to stay on my own and not become connected with any organized group. I took this to be the voice of God.

Kauai had a beneficial effect on my own physical and emotional health. Within a few months I felt on top of the world. My double vision only occurred if I was very tired and my short-term memory improved greatly though it was several more years before it would be entirely restored. I continued to practice focusing energy on my own body parts that needed attention and was thrilled to discover that I could visit clients from a distance to accomplish healing work.

Arthur was the client who brought that realization to me. When he came to see me he was still suffering from injuries he had sustained in a road accident a few years earlier. He had head problems, lack of focus and drifting sensations. I gave him a healing session in which I was surprised to discover a trapped pocket of fluid lodged in his brain – a condition I would see many times in various clients over the years.

Two days after our session, Arthur called. While on the phone I pictured his brain, wondering how the healing was going. I found that I was not only picturing this pocket clearly, but also feeling it. There was still a small amount of fluid, which I moved along with my energy tool. When I say 'energy tool' I'm describing working with energy to perform operations of regeneration. It is like a very fine ray, therefore it becomes a tool. When Arthur came to see me again the following day, the area was clear. This let me know that I wasn't just imagining things on the phone. I had actually seen and worked on the fluid in his brain to good effect.

Seeing the way healing evolves is fascinating. At first, some of those early sessions could take as long as two hours. My work has now refined to enable me to complete a session by phone in fifteen minutes. Personal sessions take longer because I like my client to remain in the altered state for at least thirty minutes after I have finished my work, which takes approximately ten minutes.

Life was going well, but money was still scarce. Funds Jane had sent me from my small bank account were dwindling fast but I found it hard to accept money for healing. My parents had taught me not to expect reward for any favours for neighbours, and somehow I considered my healings in this way. I prayed often, 'Please God, show me how to earn my living from my fashion designs.' I had still not dropped my fashion plans completely so that I could heal for free. However, it seemed God had other ideas.

I had few regrets about allowing the accident settlement money to slip through my fingers. The amount awarded was to cover injuries that would last for the rest of my life, but if I had kept the money, I might have kept the injuries as well. I didn't want to feel that I had earned money that way. By using up the settlement, I had cancelled out mental blocks it might have placed in the way of regaining my health. I am much happier and stronger earning money from my work than from being a casualty of life. Victim consciousness makes people weak.

At this transformative period of my life, I was blossoming into a fully-fledged healer. It tested my faith to the utmost and at the same time I was facing my fear of going forward without money. Everything was in God's hands; I trusted that I would be provided for and I can honestly say I was never let down.

To help cover my expenses, I gave riding lessons. I was surprised and delighted to find many horses and potential riding students on Kauai. Being with horses again nurtured my soul and provided much enjoyment as well as some income. I also enjoyed sewing curtains and cushion covers to make my beach hut cosy.

Some nights, the pounding of the waves was so loud I would expect the next one to come crashing through the hut. But this never frightened me: on the contrary, it made me feel close to nature and to God. I was filled with spiritual love and gratitude.

Within four months there was a steady stream of people turning up to be healed. All of them came from personal recommendations. People were calling from the mainland of the USA saying they were coming to Kauai for a vacation and would like to see me while they were here. I was delighted. My work was growing stronger and more precise. I was fascinated by the progression – as my work improved, more people showed up at the hut to be healed and the greater my abilities and confidence became. It was a delightful upward spiral. I was never faced with a person I didn't know I could help. I truly believed that every soul wanted to be as strong and healthy as possible. I'd yet to be faced with a true victim.

By now I was seeing more of the internal body, such as major glands, during sessions. I became alarmed when sometimes my own body would react with slight pain in the coinciding area of the person I had worked on. I would be no good to anyone if I picked up my clients' pain or condition. Thus I worked to increase my concentration and to focus positive energy with enough power to block negative frequencies coming from their bodies and energy fields. It became a process of dis-empowering their negative fields so that no malign energy would invade my system. I knew nothing of intricate energy field circuitry or sympathetic resonance then, but I *had* learned that life can be compared to a music lesson.

If two people in tune with each other each held a guitar one of them could pluck a note and the other guitar would automatically resound on the same note. We come into school on the planet in our lifetime, somehow waiting to resound to the vibrational frequency of the positive God energy. However, our fields can resound to both positive and negative energy. Therefore it becomes vital to obliterate all negative energies from our lives. I called the energy field the *aura* then, though soon I was to move far beyond that stage.

I was invited to speak about energy healing at small gatherings in a client's home and these sessions went so well that I decided to give a larger one. I practised with the beach as my stage, the sea as my audience. I had flyers printed, rented a conference room that seated 100 and cost $100 for the hire and looked forward to a lively evening. But only three people showed up. I was hugely disappointed but determined not to let it throw me. Another round of talking to myself ensued. 'Robyn, you must continue. You must believe that success is failure turned inside out.' If I had not been able to handle this I could never have gone on to give successful lectures later. *Never give up*, I say.

I had come to Hawaii as the result of a sequence of events that began with a man with the right name but the wrong number. Six months later, a similar coincidence would lead me off the island to continue my journey on the mainland USA. This time, the name was wrong, the number right.

Late one afternoon, I picked up a message from someone who needed help. 'Hello, Robyn, this is Dorothy calling. I'm staying at the Papaya Beach resort. I need to see you.'

I rang the resort, but a desk clerk told me that she could not connect me unless I knew the caller's last name. Dorothy's message had sounded urgent and I had such a strong urge that I rang the hotel again. This time a more helpful operator answered, 'I think a Dorothy is in room 5211. I'll try it for you.'

A woman's voice said hello.

'Is this Dorothy?' I asked.

'No, my name is Lynn.'

My heart sank. Not knowing what to say, I blurted out, 'I work with energy for healing. Someone named Dorothy left a message on my machine. Sorry I bothered you.'

I was about to hang up when she said, 'Wait! I need you. I just found lumps in my breast. I prayed all night for someone like you.' Lynn said she knew I was the right person for her from the sound of my voice. We made an appointment for the following day. I continued to search for Dorothy, but apparently no one by that name was registered at the hotel.

When I met Lynn the first scan of her body revealed strong, healthy body parts except for her lymphatic system, which was not functioning fully. 'I suggest you learn to go with the flow of life more, then your lymph glands will execute their role correctly,' I said. I now knew that lymph glands were part of the body's drainage system and had seen that Lynn's were blocked. She was not a relaxed person. Many people with rigid personalities have blocked lymph system and kidney problems too. They tend to hang on to the inside of their bodies, drawing up the body parts, actually tightening the tissue structure.

Lynn confided that she and her husband had been

attempting to conceive a child for some time, but she was stressed because their efforts had failed so far.

I encouraged her to follow her dream. 'I'm sure if you relax more and take things as they come, it will happen.' Fortunately, the lumps were more cystic than cancerous. We had five sessions during the next ten days and the lumps started to diminish. Her energy was restored to a very high level.

Lynn was so elated by the effects of my healing that she later called from San Francisco to say that she was coordinator of a large women's yoga group and invited me there: 'Robyn, if we pay your fare, would you come over and work with us?'

Would I ever! I was delighted with the invitation and thrilled at the prospect of seeing Aaron who was in college in San Francisco. I had a few pangs over leaving Kauai, but I knew that I would take my wonderful spiritual mountains with me in my heart and hoped to return one day.

I took off for the mainland unaware that for the next two years I would face severe testing of my faith and ability to heal. If I had realized the extent and difficulty of this as I flew off I probably would not have set out. But whoever or whatever was watching over me gradually revealed the purpose of my journey one day at a time as I moved forward into the future.

This period would become my personal walkabout, a term originally used by Australian aboriginal people to describe the time when a young man would leave his tribe and venture out on his own into the unknown in order to find his true being. Self-discovery and challenge as rights of passage are as ancient as humankind. I was a woman and no youngster, but my new path required nothing less of me than a new identity. I could only come to rely upon this new self if I risked everything and set off, with faith and hope, to an uncertain future that required me to apply the knowledge I had received and to create a practical context for the metaphysical aspects of my new life.

I also needed time to reflect upon and assimilate my experiences and feelings for God as they shifted from the quasi-human father to God as pure energy. Often prospective clients would ask me, 'Do you believe in God?' before they allowed me to work on them. I felt as though I'd been stabbed. It really pained me to think that any one could not consider the positive God energy, which I used in my work, as pure. I needed mental clarity to trust that my ability to heal came from pure goodness. I needed to be so sure of myself that criticism could not derail me. Cynicism can be a high hurdle in a world bent on proving that this form of healing does not work.

Somewhere out there I would eventually find the answers and the strength I needed, but the struggle turned out to be more difficult than I could ever have imagined.

Chapter 10

Pathway Extends to Mainland USA

Aaron met me at the airport with a big hug and I looked around me excitedly as we drove into San Francisco towards the inexpensive little hotel he had booked me into. With some trepidation I told him of my success in healing people in Hawaii, but he took it in his stride and even suggested I begin to ask clients for letters of verification. Just then he and Jane were the only members of my family who showed belief in me.

After Aaron left me at the hotel I began to set up appointments for healing sessions with Lynn's yoga group. They came to my hotel room, people with minor ailments ranging from spinal weaknesses to digestive problems. Two had blood-sugar imbalances; many had emotional scarring.

Word spread and soon I found myself invited to work on new clients, often in impressive homes. San Francisco was and remains a gracious city, but many people there seemed to have markedly higher stress levels than the clients I'd worked with in Kauai. I'm sure I was guided to become aware of the difference between a relaxed body system and the extra work needed to obtain results in a hectic city. I found it difficult to get through the stress barrier of some of these people and met the challenge by going very slowly to gain complete access to their systems. I was dismayed, but realized it was just another test that I must pass. The stress fields of the city dwellers made me aware that my concentrated focus needed to become even stronger.

The quality of energy that came through to me was changing as well. I seemed to be using it by feel more than directing the ray consciously, as the white colour of the Divine. I was not having to concentrate on bringing the light into my forehead before directing it as a ray. My energy ray was ready after one deep breath, the same breath that I teach my clients to take. This breath that I always take before each session now seemed to be the key to having my ray poised and ready. But clients were beginning to appear the right way around instead of reversed, so the body of the person I was working on was mirrored in my mental visualization. It was tricky, as their left appeared to me as their right. I had to be careful when stating rights and lefts.

After four weeks in San Francisco, I decided to take up invitations from other Americans I'd met in Hawaii and set off across the USA on a path that would lead me through many states, from California to Alabama, Georgia, Tennessee, Florida and Washington. My work evolved over the months.

Most of the people I met were likeable and honest, but not always. Besides discovering more about body healing, I also learned much about human nature. A woman I'd treated in Hawaii invited me to Florida and said that she had several friends lined up for me to see. These clients would pay my airfare from San Francisco and would pay me for healing at an agreed rate. (By this time I was reluctantly charging for sessions because having put healing above all else I now had no other means of earning a living.) I was promised several people to work with, including my hostess's husband who had many minor problems. I offered to help him free of charge to cover my keep. During the two weeks of daily healing sessions with him I kept asking when the others would be starting. My hostess had a different excuse every day. The penny finally dropped and I realized that I had been duped – there *were* no other clients. When I confronted her she admitted it and told me to leave without offering me a dime. I could only afford a seat back on the Greyhound bus and throughout my journey to San Francisco I cried and thought of the cruel lesson I had learned. Or had I?

In my enthusiasm to demonstrate to the world that there is a more intelligent and gentler approach to healing, I had overlooked some pitfalls and failed to see that childlike eagerness and trust would lead me into difficult situations again. I prayed on that bus for God to show me the way, but trust in God was operating at about 85 per cent and I wanted to rely on the Infinite 100 per cent.

I wanted my family to think I was doing fine so I avoided calling to ask Jane to send money from my ever-dwindling bank account in Australia. I saved money by eating in fast-food restaurants and found that American hamburger meals provided the best nutrition for the little money I had. I must say God was always there, sometimes at the twenty-fourth hour, and I was never let down. I did a lot of thinking around that time and I've done even more since.

Maybe just then I was in danger of becoming almost paranoid as one stroke of bad luck seemed to be followed by another. In retrospect I realize that my setbacks were part of a learning curve – but it didn't feel that way at the time.

By October I was in Chattanooga, Tennessee, where I had been invited to work for several weeks at a healing centre operating from a graceful old southern mansion. I don't think that Chattanooga is widely known as a spiritual capital but it turned out to be one for me. At an energy support group one night, the chairman asked the seated circle of eight to close their eyes and relax, then to send out group energy to support each individual.

I was relaxed but not really in a meditative state when the leader said, 'okay, that's long enough.' I was just about to open my eyes when an angel appeared to me. He was huge, taller than the 20-foot ceiling, with a very handsome, clean-shaven face. Shiny dark brown hair hung to his shoulders. His wings were motionless, his feathers incredibly white. I will never forget how large and strong the muscle bulge was where those wings joined his body. To this day I don't know what that vision meant; perhaps I was just meant to have that wonderful moment and I have prayed to see the angel again.

After my time was up at the mansion, I flew to Alabama where I rented a small basement apartment from a woman named Marlene. It was November and I felt completely worn out. I knew that I had to halt my energy sessions. More than anything, my heart ached for my children and I wanted to go home to Australia for Christmas, but I was broke as usual. I had walked the streets of Chattanooga, stopping at shops, fruitlessly offering my sewing talents, but here in Alabama I landed an order to make 100 fleece jackets. It was a huge amount of work for a very low profit but it was enough money to take me to Australia for Christmas.

I borrowed a sewing-machine and turned my bedroom into a factory where I sewed for seventeen hours a day to finish the order. After buying my ticket I would be left with only $500 but that was okay, and furthermore I had come upon some unusual cotton fabric that looked perfect for a line of women's underwear. Immediately buoyant, my imagination created the designs. When I told my landlady of my idea, she volunteered to take me to see a friend who was a clothing manufacturer and might be interested.

We went to his office the following day and I told him of my design plan. He liked the idea and wanted me to sew twelve samples for him. One week later, I presented them. He was keen. 'I'll send them to my agent in New York,' he said.

I could hardly believe it. I'm going to make it in fashion yet, I thought. The man told me soon afterwards that we both stood to make a lot of money as the New York people had liked the samples. I was so trusting and naïve that I never thought of getting a letter of agreement from him. Here, once again, was a lesson I had to learn. Marlene, meanwhile, made it clear that she wanted a piece of the action for the introduction and negotiated a handsome slice of the profits.

I decided to stay in Alabama as long as possible, hoping the New York order would be placed before I left. I duly finished the jackets and was paid. I owed Marlene three weeks' rent and I wanted to stay another three weeks before I left for home. I still had the sewing-machine rental to pay for and then Marlene informed me she had decided to raise the rent three weeks before because of the extra electricity I'd used.

'But I can't get my ticket home if you do that,' I said. I begged and pleaded, but she told me I'd better pay or else. She claimed to have friends in the police department and threatened to tell them I had wrecked her furniture.

My mind was reeling. 'We made an agreement. I'm going to pay you our agreed rental and a little over for electricity, just to be fair. I'm going out now. When I return, I expect you to be decent.'

I returned, hopefully if not trustingly, to find myself locked out, my few possessions inside the apartment. *I won't be blackmailed*, I thought, *my principles will not allow it*.

Not knowing where to turn, I knocked on the neighbours' door and told them of my plight. 'She does that to all the people she rents to, always blackmailing them for more money. We wanted to warn you. We'll call the police for you,' they said. 'You stay here until they arrive.' At least some people could be kind and decent.

I found my luggage dumped on Marlene's front path and then the police arrived. 'She always does things like this,' the police confirmed. 'Do you want to press charges?'

'No,' I said sadly, handing them some money. 'Just see she gets this rent I owe.' They drove me to a motel. Now, having to pay motel rates, I thought I'd never afford my ticket. *At least you have your self-worth*, I thought to myself, absolutely determined to resist self-pity. I remembered I still had an antique gold and multi-coloured pearl necklace and I sold it to buy my ticket home. At that point, seeing my family was all that mattered.

But it was a terrible Christmas. I was not welcomed or congratulated as I had somehow, maybe unrealistically, expected. I knew of the good work I had accomplished but my family imagined I had been on a giant, self-indulgent holiday. They were not even willing to read the letters clients had given me, attesting my healing ability. At last Jane did read them. 'I'm sure you can do it,' she said, 'But why you, Mum?'

I could not answer. I realized that it was difficult for them to understand that people can be healed with energy and to comprehend why their mother chose to be a pioneer. I could hardly believe it myself and yet at some profound level I knew that I was directed to the USA because my own country was not ready for the concept of energy healing. I needed fieldwork and lots of bodies and energies to work with. The American people were ready, a huge percentage of them already sought natural healing methods to blend with conventional healing. Australia on the other hand has a very small population and at that time it was still very pro orthodox medicine. I believe attitudes are changing.

I stayed on in Sydney with two dear friends but by March 1995 I was pining to return to America. Once again, my feelings were too strong to fight.

Another man whose name began with 'R' had come on the scene. I met Rick in Seattle. He had wanted me to stay, offering me a room in his home. I'd wanted to keep moving at the time but he promised me I could stay if I returned there. I didn't see him as a romantic prospect, but he seemed a kind gentleman. His assurance of a place to stay if I returned to the USA enabled me to plan my return. I knew that this meant having to establish myself as a healer from a firm base but that was a challenge I was happy to meet as Seattle seemed open and ready for alternative methods. I could not have faced the worry of having nowhere to stay. At times in the past insecurity had been a huge test of my faith and I felt I could not go through it again. This alone proved that my faith in God was not yet 100 per cent.

Scraping up enough money for a ticket and living expenses was my major concern. By now, I knew that my underwear designs would not pay off: I had tried many times to call the manufacturer in Alabama, but with no response. Hopelessness and despair all but overcame me. I had nothing to fall back on – but at least I had a place to stay.

My only hope of finding the fare lay with a small gold investment I had made in 1988. It should have brought huge returns, but I only recovered one-third of my stake. I refused to give in to self-pity, preferring to focus on the fact that I now had enough money to fly back to America. I felt frightened about my ability to survive on such a small amount, but tried to plan how I could manage my finances. I purchased some small opals to sell later. By the time I had paid for a one-way ticket, I had little left. I kept phoning Rick for reassurance about the Seattle room.

Meanwhile I had met Thomas in Sydney. I both liked and pitied him. He made a wonderful, natural body-moisturizing oil but had not been able to sell it in Australia. I told him I would try to market it in San Francisco for a percentage of sales. I was stopping over there to see my son and felt that the shops could go for Thomas's product. That would give me a small income: I still had a problem accepting money for healing.

I left for San Francisco and returned to the small hotel where my son was again able to arrange a favourable rate. I started calling beauty shops to make appointments and had to work fast as I'd only planned to be there for a week before flying to Seattle. What a gamble! The proprietor of one shop seemed interested and the next day he confirmed they would place an order the following Wednesday, with a cash advance. This meant staying another week, however, which I could not afford.

That evening, a woman I had met the year before in Kauai called and asked me to work on her friend's tailbone, which was slowly crippling her. The problem was a small cat-like tail growing from the base of the coccyx. She lived an hour away and invited me to stay at her home while I worked on her friend.

Perfect! I could move out of the hotel and accept a little money for healing. Everything was falling into place. I could stay there for the week and return to San Francisco to take the order.

The house was beautiful and I felt quite happy with my old acquaintance from Kauai. Her friend and I sat together and I began to scan her. When I reached the end of her spine, I saw the small curved tail, which tipped sharply to the left. It was gristle, not bone, approximately one-eighth of an inch thick. I used the energy ray to push very slowly straight through and sever it. This was the first dissection I had carried out. I transported it away from the area so it could be eradicated from her body. (At that time I always transported waste tissues to the bowel area where they could be eliminated easily by the body. I don't do this any more, as damaged tissue seems to disintegrate into body waste automatically.) The following day's session showed swelling which was also apparent on the outside of the client's coccyx. I was pleased that inside the area looked clean and was already showing signs of healing. After two more sessions, she was well on the way to total health.

I returned to the city elated. I would pick up the money and be on my way to Seattle. But the order was delayed for three more days. How I hated that seemingly eternal financial cliff-edge! Then, when I called Rick, he told me he had fallen in love. He was sorry, but his girlfriend did not want another woman in the apartment.

I was shattered. But even without Rick's support, I somehow knew I had to get to Seattle. Thomas in Australia could only help a little with the hotel bill and by now I really had the shakes. Thoughts of returning home crossed my mind but then an overwhelming surge of positive energy ran through me. *You said you were going back to Seattle and my God, you are going to do it.*

When I got to the beauty shop I waited for the owner to speak. 'We can't place an order just now,' he said weakly.

Tears welled up. 'But you promised. I was relying on the advance from your order for my ticket.' He must have felt guilty that I had waited around for a week because he bought me the plane ticket and I was able to fly out that day. On the way to the airport, the bus passed through areas where street people hung out. *My God, is this where I am heading?* Anxiety started to overwhelm me. *No, you said you were going to Seattle, now do it.* The problem was I'd be arriving there at the start of a long weekend with very little money and no place to go. I decided that the best thing to do would be to stay in the airport for the next three days.

I climbed off the plane looking like a million dollars in the glamorous travel outfit I had copied from one Sharon Stone wore in a film, proudly topped by a great hat. But it made me conspicuous and I knew the law did not like people loitering at airports. I was virtually destitute so if apprehended I would have to say that I had lost my return ticket to Australia and was waiting for money to be sent.

The airport had a wonderful meditation room where I hid. On the second day, I met the airport minister. If she thought I was in trouble she kept quiet, and no one would have guessed my predicament by looking at me. That same afternoon a young man who reminded me of my son came by. He told the minister and me that he was stuck, lacking 40 dollars for a ticket to Toronto. He said he had wanted to surprise his mother by booking himself into Washington State University while she was away in Germany. He had even tried to get a few hours' work in the airport coffee shop. If he did not return today, his visa would expire and his university dream would be shattered. My heart lurched: if Aaron were in trouble like this, I would want someone to help him. I gave him 40 dollars, which left me with 60 dollars and three opals.

That night, as I sat on a bench in the restroom, I watched a woman fight tears as she washed her hands. 'Are you okay?' I asked.

'No, not really,' she said. 'I am not well but I'm hoping to have enough strength to get on the plane to see my dying mother.'

'I have come to Seattle to perform healing work,' I said. 'Would you like a session?'

'Oh, how wonderful, please,' she answered. We sat together and I scanned her body. Besides psychological heartache, she had a heart malfunction which I corrected during the session.

Forty minutes later she said, 'I feel stronger, let me give you some money.' I refused, but she insisted, pushing bills at me and into my pocket. I took her to the gate where we hugged goodbye, both crying with relief. She was better. And I was 110 dollars richer.

Using up cash on an airport locker and the bus fare into town, I went to the university area where I remembered several jewellery shops from my last trip and hoped someone would buy my opals. The first jeweller informed me that my best stone had a crack. This happens sometimes with climate change. None of the other shops was interested. It took me all my strength to hold myself together. My legs felt weak and I shook inside. I saw a travel agency and went in to ask the price of a return ticket to Australia. I don't know why, as I had no money for it.

A young man there heard my accent. 'I'm here collecting my ticket to go to your country,' he said.

'Really, what do you do?' I asked.

'I'm an energy worker,' he said.

With that, my tears flowed. I found myself pouring out my troubles to him, including the fact that I had no place to stay.

'No problem,' he said. He picked up the phone and soon a woman came to pick me up. A ground angel had saved me again. They were always there in my journey's darkest hours.

I never saw Steven again but over the next few months three different wonderful women let me stay with them and I was able to repay them by giving them healing sessions. The relief of having these ground angels care for me was indescribable. Such goodness more than counterbalances the hard luck. In fact maybe the hard luck can sometimes lead to these encounters with ground angels.

I was invited to a Native American ceremony by one of

my new friends. There I met Jenny who had a house to share. She needed healing, and loved opals, so she bought my stones. The house was in a beautiful neighbourhood. At last I was able to settle into my healing work and felt so at home in Seattle that I would make it my home and stay there for years.

Chapter 11

Perils of the Journey

Safe in Seattle, I relaxed and enjoyed serenity I had not known for a long time. Six weeks after my arrival I heard a radio interview with Dr Valerie Hunt, a researcher on human energy fields with degrees in psychology and physiology. Her talk was so interesting that I ran to tape it. She was discussing her new book, *Infinite Mind: Science of the Human Vibrations of Consciousness*. As I listened to Dr Hunt talk about her research at the University of California, my heart raced. Her scientific studies of energy fields confirmed everything I knew intuitively.

The following day I bought her book and read it avidly. Dr Hunt had used telemetry instruments, developed by the National Aeronautics and Space Administration, to measure the body's electrical activity. She measured not only the electrical current of the nervous system, brain neurons and nerves, but also the 'human energy field, the pool of electromagnetic energy around an object or a person that allows energy exchange'.

I was thrilled to read:

Although composed of the same electrons as inert substances, the human field absorbs and throws off energy dynamically. It interacts with and influences matter, whereas fields associated with inert matter react passively. Again, there have been many names associated with this human energy: chi, life force, prana, odic force and aura.

During my journey towards healing, I had often been asked if I worked with the aura or with the seven chakra energy centres described in Hindu texts. I explained that aura is the name we first gave to the human energy field, but my work is more intensive now that I understand more and can actually readjust the frequency pattern of these fields for maximum energy output. I get better results when I close my eyes. Aura healers use their hands, and I do not, which demonstrates that my work is different from the others'. Somehow, the chakra concepts did not seem to mesh with the healing lessons that were coming through to me.

Dr Hunt's findings made more sense. She had discovered that each person has a unique energy field that shows areas where energy flows more freely while others are blocked. Measuring various systems of the body, she found that 'changes occurred in the field before any of the other systems changed'. She went on to say, 'As a result of my work, I can no longer consider the body as organic systems or tissues. The healthy body is a flowing, interactive electrodynamic energy field.'

As I continued with my life and healing sessions, I reflected on Dr Hunt's book, especially the charts that showed the shape of waves in the energy field as revealed by her laboratory instruments. If it was indeed true that a person's energy field carries the ultimate level of information, then I wanted to work with energy fields in healing.

I began visualizing the graphs of the human energy field in her book and could picture the circuits in my clients' fields. Three weeks later, I was including the human energy field in my sessions. I could see it in graphic detail, often including colour.

I cannot say precisely how it came about that I obtained accurate, useful information in this way. Perhaps I was accessing the same mysterious process I had discovered when I spontaneously used the information in Lobsang Rampa's *The Third Eye* to focus an energy ray to heal myself when I had the tumour. It seemed that anything I could visualize, I could manifest in my work.

Around this time my healing work really began to take off. Within a short time I became proficient at reading the field. Word of mouth brought clients to me. With the inclusion of the energy field, my sessions gradually became more powerful and I was able to develop a fairly standard way to work on my clients. Having a regular clientele, I was now seeing new glands daily and more of the nerve system during my scans.

The energy field we live in is very large, sometimes more than 40 feet in diameter. Negative thoughts and feelings look like dirty, snowy obstructions. In my sessions, I always clear the field of negative energies to set up a positive energy flow. After clearing emotional negativity, I read the field on the left side at ground level. Here I can tell the condition of the blood, cells, and tissue. I work through this first body quarter to the elbow. All weaknesses in this area will show up as snow. If there is biological weakness, I strengthen the energy circuits and clear any snow.

Clearance is easy but if the mental or physical cause is not dealt with, circuitry breakdown will recur.

Then I work from the elbow to the top of the crown of the head. This quarter of the energy field shows the strength of the heart, or generator, as I prefer to call it. The chest and upper lymphatic gland system show here as well as the shoulder, upper arm and upper vertebrae. I then scan over the head to reveal any head trauma. The journey continues down the right side. The first quarter reveals the upper glands, liver and gall bladder, pancreas, spleen, stomach, adrenals, kidneys, colon, female or male reproductive system, bladder and urinary tract. The lower spine is also included. Legs show up in the lower sections of the field.

Once I complete the silent scan and clearing of the energy field, I ask my client for permission to enter their body, where I work on all the unwell areas found in their energy field. I actually see the organs, glands, bones and all other body parts. They appear to me just as they would look in a photograph, though sometimes they are not completely clear. It's dark inside the body and colour can be difficult to discern, always appearing dull if an area is in trouble. I repair body parts using energy. You might suppose that it would be impossible actually to see colour, but there is no doubt in my mind that I can.

I can use the energy tool in many ways. If I use it as a broom and just lovingly sweep with it, the energy ray fans out and expands. I can use it as a rake when I'm clearing away debris in the field, clearing out little gremlin frequencies. I can use it as a hook to pull things; I can use it as a scalpel for delicate surgery. It's the same wave of energy but I can use the tool differently. Some operations are so delicate that I bring it down to the size of a fine-point pen. I try to avoid using the energy as a scalpel. If there's another way, I will try it first.

Regeneration is accomplished by using the ray as a very fine but very forceful tool that reaches to the depths of body parts. This is accomplished by focusing the ray powerfully into the depths of any body part that becomes strong enough to accept it. Early in my healing journey, I discovered that I was able to function simultaneously on multi-dimensional levels. During a session on Kauai, while easing a neck vertebra back into position, I was holding a conversation with my woman client. It then struck me that I was talking on the third earthly dimension and yet working with fifth dimension-focused energy.

Too much chatter charged with nervous energy can cause minor blockage and indicates that the client is not fully receiving my work, so I knew that day that I must function on these different levels. The process evolved so that I was able to converse both verbally to the client and telepathically to body parts simultaneously, either in person or on the telephone.

I work the same way in telephone sessions as I do in person. Whether the client is in a chair next to me or on a distant continent, I see and heal them in the same way, first removing negative energy from the field and replacing it with huge amounts of positive energy, then entering the body and working with my energy tool.

I believe that as we evolve, the ability I have will be available to most healers.

My housemate and new friends in Seattle told their friends about the healing they had received and word spread. One of my first clients was Eva, who had been sick as the result of chemical poisoning for fifteen years. She became ill while working at a nursery that used toxic chemical sprays on the plants, particularly poinsettias. While she was working in the nursery, Eva's house was being insulated and the materials contained formaldehyde, so she was being poisoned both at work and at home.

'I got weaker and weaker,' Eva told me. 'I was cold most of the time, my skin turned yellow, and I had trouble working. Even an easy task like taking a phone order, was almost impossible to accomplish.'

Eva went to two different doctors and they agreed that she had an underactive thyroid. One of the physicians thought she was dying. The medication she received caused excruciating headaches and Eva had to stop taking it. Eventually she became so weak that she could not work. A practitioner of Chinese medicine found that her liver had been damaged by poisons and placed her on a stringent diet of rice and chicken. He was able to improve her health somewhat with acupuncture and herbs.

By now Eva was so sensitive that she could not tolerate exhaust fumes, perfumes, smoke, or any of the day-to-day chemicals found in the city. She and her husband were forced to move to an island away from all pollution. There she had days when she'd think she was better, but whenever she left the island, she'd encounter some smell or chemical and have serious reactions.

'I'd be disoriented or feel that my blood was running hot through my veins, or suddenly my muscles would weaken. I'd usually come down with a toxic headache the next day. The right side of my head felt as though it were contracting severely, almost like labour pains.'

By the time Eva saw me, she had been to chiropractors,

had taken instructions in Jin Shin Jyutsu, Reiki and Tai Chi, and had even tried counselling sessions, but nothing gave her much relief. The week before she came to me, her doctor had called with her latest test results: her blood pressure was much too high and she had a 95 per cent chance of suffering a heart attack or stroke.

Eva's husband drove two hours to get her to me. She was a sick woman but very cooperative. As we sat side by side, I scanned her energy field and found it very tired and stressed, full of snow. She had been badly affected not only by chemical poisons but also by electrical pollution. Her glandular system had broken down, tired of working twenty-four hours each day fighting off the invasion of chemicals that caused negative energy. Like other clients with worn-out glands, Eva's hormonal system was also in trouble. I found chemical toxins in the bronchial tubes and lung tissue. With the build-up of chemicals in those tissues, every breath she took was poisoning her.

I sent energy to the electrical circuits in her field and to her glands, then went to work on her bronchial tubes and lung tissue. Using my energy scalpel, I lifted off the tissue damaged by poisons, leaving fresh tissue exposed. I fully expected further toxins to rise to the surface of those tissues and continued removing them with my energy scalpel in subsequent sessions.

Afterwards Eva reported that her blood pressure came down, and after the second session she called to tell me her good news. 'I awoke knowing that a shift has taken place. I feel a sense of wellness I haven't experienced in fifteen years.'

Eva came to me seven times. At the end she wrote me a lovely note saying, 'I am now enjoying eating a wonderful variety of food and am able to go places without reacting to the odours around me. I feel like part of life instead of being on the outside looking in. I am filled with hope for the future and enjoying such positive energy.'

Around that time, I presented a seminar on energy healing where I met Ruth, who was sitting at the back, swathed in sheeting to keep chemicals off. She had suffered from chronic fatigue for ten years and her energy was so low that her ability to work and enjoy life was severely impaired. Like Eva, she had multiple chemical sensitivities that had led to neurological symptoms. She'd also been diagnosed with multiple sclerosis.

Ruth came to me for private healing sessions. I wasn't able to cure the MS completely but after ten sessions over two weeks, Ruth reported that she felt like 'a new person.' Two months later she reported that she was still making progress and was now able to fight the condition more effectively, needing only half the anti-viral supplements she'd been taking.

Before long other clients with chemical poisoning turned to me. Some had heard about Eva, some had learned about me from seminar attendees and others came quite mysteriously. As I mentioned earlier, I often have runs of clients with the same ailment, as if God is bringing them to me to sharpen a particular knowledge and skill.

A year and a half after I settled in Seattle, I felt secure enough to find a house of my own, the first I'd had in four years of wandering. The open-minded attitude towards alternative health in the USA was so enlightening, and my bouts of homesickness were balanced by the satisfaction of being accepted as an energy healer. The USA is undoubtedly leading the world towards spirituality and natural healing. It was gratifying to see my clients recovering and my own skill developing at the same time.

Augusta was sixty-three and had suffered from severe arthritis for fifteen years. She had recently bought a wheelchair. In the first six months of our sessions I was able to regenerate her painful hips and knees, restoring 80 per cent of her range of motion. Then I set about strengthening her entire bone structure, renewing almost every joint in her body. Her crippled fingers straightened enough to enable her to sew and play the piano again. I also restored her liver function, improving her overall health. She wrote that she felt 'energized and younger'. By the time we finished Augusta had the joints of a twenty-year-old and looked radiant. She abandoned her wheelchair and lived a normal life.

Stewart came with multiple chemical sensitivities and allergies to more than 100 substances. He believed that most of his problems were due to pre-natal exposure to DES, a synthetic female hormone erroneously thought to prevent miscarriages. I detected major problems with Stewart's glands and set about detoxing and regenerating them. After this I focused on his leg, which had been broken twenty years earlier and had never healed properly. He had a spiral fracture about 3 inches above his left ankle and it was still bruised on both sides. His leg became nearly normal and Stewart headed off to the racquetball court for the first time in twenty years.

Thrilled, we decided to try to regenerate the top joint of Stewart's little finger, which had been cut off in a doorjamb when he was two years old. Now, forty-three years later, we seemed to be growing the end of the finger. Stewart had an X-ray to discover whether we were making progress, and this showed that the bone was definitely growing. The regeneration went slowly, as we'd expected, but eventually he grew a new nail bed. He did not grow a nail, but the regeneration of missing bone and tissue was still exciting for both of us.

I'd had such success working with my clients that I was beginning to think I could regenerate anything, but my next case gave me a more realistic perspective. Sally had had a cancerous thyroid gland removed before she came to me. During the first body scan, I saw that there were a few remaining healthy cells, perhaps enough to regrow the thyroid. When I spoke with the cells, they were responsive and excited at the possibility of growing into a whole new gland.

Sally came for her second session, but before we began, she said she wanted to have a serious talk. She didn't want a new thyroid gland. She was afraid, believing that if it grew back it might become cancerous again. I was disappointed of course, but it was a good lesson for me and it came at the right time. Understanding the importance of the client's positive mental attitude and willingness to heal was essential to my work.

By now I was communicating clearly with body organs and glands and actually heard them answering. It may seem bizarre to many of you that body parts have a conscious awareness, but why not? Isn't everything connected? Why are so many disbelieving of the quiet internal language and communication? My guess is that most people can't relate to anything unless it's hard, visible, tangible. The response I get from the inside of a body simply by communicating with its parts is remarkable. It's as if, at last, someone can see them and is recognizing that they live here usually with no reward for the hard work they do every second to maintain the life of the owner. Having the ability to see inside the energy field and body has certainly been the major factor in the success of my work but I realize that some readers may need further convincing, which is why I offer the background which follows. Believe me, these conversations have been crucial to my success as a healer, to say nothing of the thrill of knowing that body parts have the ability to converse in their own simple manner.

Thus at this point I would like to share some of the conversations I've had with body parts. Kidneys and the pituitary gland are extremely communicative. The pituitary takes on the personality of its owner up to the age of seven. If the person was shy or retiring this gland usually will not be working 100 per cent. When I strengthen it to full power, the confidence of the person soon improves. The gland seems to take on tremendous responsibility for the well-being of the body. If it's shy on my first visit, it certainly changes by the second because it knows my work is helping and welcomes me with open arms, so to speak, quite often reminding me of a friendly puppy wagging its tail. I just love its character and, as I have said, it has become probably my favourite body part. I also see it as the electrical substation for brain waves.

If parts respond telepathically, it's usually in short words and phrases, such as, *I'm sick*, *I'm happy*, *I'm unhappy*, *I'm tired* or *I'm well*. However, some have answered in short sentences. Bear in mind that these responses have come from very sensitive bodies. One woman client had a very talkative body. She came for sessions shortly after having a hysterectomy and was now very upset with herself for listening to medical advice that because she already had children, she did not need these parts any more. She was having tremendous emotional upsets within. My plan was to try to boost her glandular system to promote some hormonal balance.

I was horrified to note in my first scan that the surgeon's scalpel had removed a very important gland low within the reproductive area. Why, I'll never know. So I asked the gland below if it would work harder to compensate. It seemed to agree. I waited in eager anticipation to go in the following day but upon reaching it, I felt confusion.

'Why are you unsure?' I asked.

It answered, 'How can I do this? It's different from the support I already give to the gland below me.'

I explained I could divide it with energy to enable it to play both roles. I then felt waves of fear coming from it. 'What's wrong now?' I asked.

'If I take over the role of the missing gland above me, I may be cut out also.'

I convinced it that the client would under no circumstance go under the knife again and it took over the role of the missing gland.

So who says that our body parts don't have intelligence and feelings? Another client, also from the USA, had part of her bowel removed. Doctors were not able to find the answer to fluid being expelled from the remaining organ. It had been occurring for six months. On my third visit, I asked it what the problem was. This was the answer: 'As the eyes cry tears, I am crying, also.' This bowel was having problems coping with the loss of its whole.

Asking for support from compatible glands to help weakened areas is not uncommon in my work but strange as it may seem, the glands can sometimes act sulkily, resisting my requests by telling me, 'I have enough work of my own to perform.' Then I have to scan, hoping to find another compatible gland for the job needed.

Nerves can be super-sensitive in much the same way, but usually they are very sweet to work with, especially those in the head. They speak in very short sentences consisting of no more than five or six words. Though every body responds in some way when spoken to, not all body parts reply. Women's body parts are the chattiest. When I run into a reluctance to communicate, it is usually connected to the client's 'internals' being reserved and needing time to develop trust. This is completely natural. Usually by the second or third session they give me total access to their systems, although there is no doubt that some people's body parts have the ability to communicate better than others.

I applaud the people I work with for their willingness to open up. Having a stranger enter one's psychic and physical space is a new experience for most people and may be frightening at first. Only clients' trust allows me access. Those who are spiritual are usually the easiest to work with, having positive mental attitudes, and their body parts are more willing to respond. I've discovered that no matter what their age, the tissues of their bodies tend to be flexible, springy and more receptive, having qualities usually associated with youth.

An open, clear mental attitude is needed to get results. A

good attitude helps clients maintain a positive electrical field, and a strong, clear field is necessary for ongoing recovery and health. I teach my clients how to work on themselves to achieve a positive attitude, but not everyone wants to take the trouble to do this. Many people allow negative thoughts and feelings free rein instead of taking the reprogramming breaths during the twenty second period before the electricity from then enters their energy field. Some people are wedded to the idea of some magical quick fix and want me to do everything for them.

Without a positive attitude, wellness may not last long. I encourage my clients to sort out their lifestyle. Open your eyes in the morning to ask, 'Is anything in my life making me unhappy?' If the answer is yes, you must work it out. If it's a relationship you're not sure of, place a set of scales in your mind's eye. If the scales are tipping to the positive, stay and work out ways to freshen it. If the scales tip to the negative, leave. Don't worry about money. If the person with whom you are in a negative relationship is supporting you, find a way to support yourself. The unhappiness it's causing you is breaking down your energy field circuitry which, in time, can cause serious illness. If it's a job you don't like, leave. If it's an area you live in, move.

You have to seek happiness for wellness because it keeps your generator working for positive energy. The next thing you do on opening your eyes is to tell yourself, 'Today, I'm going to have a totally positive day.' This is hard to accomplish in the beginning but things improve if you keep at it.

As I have often said, reprogramming negative thoughts and feelings can be achieved by taking a deep breath, holding air for ten seconds, then blowing it out with full force from the mouth. We only have twenty seconds to achieve this. After that, negativity has electrical power in our field circuits. As you become better at reprogramming, you will be able to restart the electrical generator, your heart, with feelings of love. Remember, our body can only tolerate one form of energy at a time, so keep it positive. Love, love and listen to the teachings of Jesus.

Clients may actually manifest new problems if sickness has become a way of life for them and they depend on it for sympathy or attention. Many mature people may take on the victim role to receive attention not given to them in childhood. True victims are impossible to heal. They have a death wish.

Death wishes can lie low. It took one woman client two years to fully realize she had a death wish. The seed had been sown years before and now it had to be turned round. She has done this and is now fine.

I cannot play God. If someone wants to die or has fulfilled their time on earth, nothing will save them. Fortunately, most people who come to be healed are willing to work at maintaining a positive outlook. As many as 90 per cent of my clients benefit from our sessions.

Chapter 12

Building on Success

After dealing with a series of chemically sensitive cases, I saw several clients who complained of a range of problems in their heads. Some had sustained injuries to their skulls, some suffered from headaches, others experienced psychological problems. Often, physical and psychological damage came together. Many of these clients were taking Prozac or other psychoactive drugs. Drugs of any sort and over-consumption of alcohol lower the intensity of glandular activity and the electrical circuits in the energy field and affect our neurology.

Overdoses nearly always show up as snow in the field; the density of the snow indicates how overdosed the clients are. As my clients begin to heal, I ask them to decrease medications gradually until they do not require drugs any more, and soon the snow clears.

Louise and her friend drove six hours to get to me. Louise was quite pretty but looked so unsure of herself that she reminded me of a frightened rabbit. This forty-five-year-old woman told me that she started having migraines when she was nine. She was in her teens before she saw a doctor for them. By then she had chronic sinusitis, so the diagnosis of what type of headache she suffered was unclear. She started taking aspirin with codeine regularly. Often she had to be taken to casualty when codeine gave her no relief. Stronger medications were administered but she was never admitted to hospital.

When she was twenty, Louise was sent to a psychiatrist because of anxiety and depression. Though chronic pain and codeine were the primary causes of her depression, her visits to psychiatrists continued on and off for many years. The doctors gave her anti-depressants and anti-anxiety medications and asked her to dig into her psyche for deep, dark secrets that might explain her mental state. Though no psychological cause for her headaches was unearthed, Louise began to doubt her sanity.

In her thirties, she started treatment with a neurologist who put her on vasoconstrictors, calcium channel blockers and strong pain medications containing sedatives. 'I felt like a walking zombie,' Louise said as she told me her history, 'But I somehow managed to hold down a very good job as a technical editor.'

Eventually the pressure of her job got the better of her. Her migraines raged out of control and she was 'crazy with the pain'. She couldn't sleep or eat, her weight dropped below 100 pounds. Her neurologist wanted to hospitalize her and hook her up to a constant IV drip of vaso-constrictors, pain medication and sedatives. Louise refused. She left her job and was put on medical disability allowance. Three years later she was able to work at a less stressful job, but even that was difficult. Her self-esteem and confidence had sunk to an all-time low.

Meanwhile, other medical problems showed up each

time she visited the doctor. She had unspecific anaemia that doctors could not explain or successfully treat. She developed hypothyroidism, but when she started taking thyroid medication her pituitary shut down. They were worried that she would suffer from bone-marrow loss if she continued on the pituitary medication. By April 1998, Louise was at the bottom of the world. Her marriage was under strain, she could barely care for her two young sons and she was extremely depressed. Her primary care physician said he wanted to start over as if she were a new case and recommended costly lab tests.

Louise decided that if she was to try again, she would start on a new spiritual path. Her faith in God, her prayers and those of others kept her going. 'Finally, I surrendered my life and my body to God. Only God knows how to heal them,' she told me. She believed that God had led her to me.

Louise came to me for thirteen sessions over two months. I was able to relieve her pain and to remove drugs she'd taken for more than thirty years out of her system. It's amazing how quickly the dosage of drugs can be lowered and then eliminated once weakness or injuries are tended and repaired.

Afterwards, in a thank-you note, she said, 'I'm practically pain-free and getting stronger every day. I'm enjoying my children and my husband, and our family is healing as well.'

A variety of things may be responsible for weaknesses in the head area, the most common being injury from accidents or births involving forceps and the like. Quite often the client does not remember the injury and has no idea how it happened. Some injuries may have occurred thirty or forty years before our meeting. I obtain this information from the brain itself or from the energy field. Once I tell people what I've discovered, they often remember the incident or get corroboration from relatives.

Scar tissue grows in the body to protect damaged areas but sometimes it does not know when to stop. It keeps growing and damages arteries, capillaries and nerves in the head and reminds me of ivy on a tree. Overdeveloped scar tissue in the head can hinder the normal flow of blood and fluid, known as cerebrospinal fluid, and impair nerve action. In many clients with head problems I found trapped pockets of fluid deep in their brains, caused by injuries to the head. If the head is operating correctly, I can see fluid flowing in a neat, symmetrical pattern, reaching every area of the brain. But when the head has been traumatized it often looks as though the tide has gone out, leaving little pockets of fluid, perhaps not more than a quarter-teaspoon-ful, trapped in places. They may seem insignificant, but they create enormous problems. They may be responsible for light-headedness, impaired balance and memory loss and focus.

When I encounter pockets of fluid, I move the fluid along to drain at the front of the head through the sinuses or through the lymphatic glands at the back. I use my energy ray with a pulling motion to suction out the fluid and send it towards the drainage channels. Then I go back over the area from the top and use a sweeping motion to make sure the fluid is gone. I usually get it out in one session. When their head fluids flow correctly, clients quickly regain full control of their mental faculties.

When I work on brain function I can strengthen the

pituitary gland, located deep in the base of the brain. The pituitary is like a signal box; it's the electrical substation of the brain. All brain signals go through that gland. Its other roles include regulating the activity of other endocrinal glands. No bigger than a small grape, it is probably my favourite body part. I call it Captain, as it takes on so much responsibility for the wellness of the complete body. When it knows my work is responsible for this wellness, it gives me a huge welcome.

As I have said, the pituitary takes on the personality that the client had before the age of seven. When I bring a weak pituitary gland up to full strength, I not only send it energy to make it stronger physically, I actually communicate with it to give it confidence. Within months, with the pituitary and both sides of the brain working correctly, the client becomes confident and self-assured.

I discovered while working on healing myself that the brain is the slowest part of the body to respond. Severe head problems usually take several months to clear up after healing sessions. Without these, however, brain function may never be restored.

John came to me after suffering for twenty years with discomfort and mental distress associated with hypo-glycaemia, or low blood-sugar. When he was first diag-nosed with hypoglycaemia at the age of thirty, he tried to control it by eating more protein and staying away from refined sugars. Proper nutrition helped, but sometimes he didn't feel he was functioning at full capacity. When he felt irritable he would withdraw instead of taking out his feelings on others because he knew that it was spiritually incorrect to punish any living thing in this way. But his apparent detachment was also stressful and damaging to his relationships.

In spite of careful diet, John's symptoms gradually worsened. By the time he was fifty, even the sugar from a piece of fruit could upset his precarious chemical balance. He would feel queasy and even the gentle motion of turning his head could bring on a bout of dizziness. John was the editor of an alternative health magazine and so had access to both orthodox and unconventional health services, but nothing he'd tried had given him permanent relief. Finally, an employee of a medical clinic referred him to me, and he drove 60 miles to my home.

John had done much work on himself, spiritually and emotionally, and when we sat together he went into the altered state very quickly. When I scanned through his brain, I noticed a pocket containing about a teaspoonful of fluid in the middle near the hypothalamus. I could see that John had hit his head quite hard many years before and the blow had resulted in the formation of this pocket. I focused my energy ray and opened the pocket gently, then moved the fluid along so that it could drain out slowly. I realized that when the fluid drained out, the lymph glands at the back of the crown would swell up, and reassured him that it was part of the healing process.

After our session, John confirmed that he had indeed hit his head in a motorcycle accident at the age of twenty, but had never associated that accident with his hypoglycaemia. The accident had taken place during his adult life so John could remember feeling normal before he was injured and called on those memories to accelerate the healing process.

He returned for two more sessions and by the third, I saw that all the fluid was gone. As I'd predicted, lymph glands on the sides of his neck swelled from the drainage, but these gradually diminished. He had researched and discovered that one of the functions of the hypothalamus is regulation of autonomic functions of the body like blood-sugar and the insulin hormones.

Like all my clients, John felt tired after our sessions and rested for several days. He believed that it was his body's way of incorporating the healing energy and perhaps releasing toxins.

I was delighted when he sent me a letter stating that his energy had increased so much that he felt like a teenager again. He went on to say, 'I now work on my own body, and have included talking and sending love to glands and organs into my own healing work with others. Now, six months later, I feel free of the mental distress that would come on me, the dizziness, the low blood-sugar . . . I have done visualization even more now, and my body feels wonderful, and so do my mind and soul.'

As a healer, I could not ask for more from a client. I wish everyone took their abilities to heal themselves as seriously as John did and continued to visualize their body parts and work on themselves. Before you go to sleep sometimes, particularly after your body has worked hard and well for you, with your eyes closed, send a surge of warm positive energy through it, even stopping along the way to thank major parts individually. I must admit when I first did this it sounded humorous as I said, 'Thank you, heart, thank you, liver.' It was as though my whole insides had the giggles. Yet many of my clients receive, as I do, a flutter of response from recognized parts.

These days I say, 'Thanks, team, you got me through another day and worked so hard.' You will be amazed at

how much better your body will work once you give these
wonderful components recognition. Don't forget they are
in there slogging away, trying so hard to fulfill their role,
just to keep you living. So, thank them, please.

My next client was Edward, an attorney in his fifties. When
he showed up, I saw only a well-dressed businessman; there
was no external evidence of his head injuries. I knew from
my own experience that head injuries may not show – when
I suffered from double vision my eyes had looked perfectly
normal to others even though I felt I must look cross-eyed.

Edward told me that in 1993 he'd been hospitalized with
a sub-arachnoid haemorrhage, or bleeding in the back of the
head which neurosurgeons described as potentially life-
threatening. Pain and nausea began while he was jogging
one morning and he got to the hospital quickly. A CAT scan
indicated leakage of blood and an MRI confirmed a considerable amount of blood pooled around the brain stem.
Doctors could not find the source of the leakage and after
four days in hospital Edward was feeling well enough to be
released. He believed that his prayers and the prayers of his
wife and friends had fixed the problem, but he went on to
experience periods of disorientation that grew worse over
time.

Edward came to see me in April 1999. He reported
being so disoriented some days that he felt as though his
'mind was turning inside out'. Edward went on, 'It is a
tremendous strain to attempt to keep my focus and
maintain my balance and stability during these episodes.
I cannot concentrate for extended periods, which makes
working at my law practice extremely difficult. I also
experience short-term memory loss to the extent that I

can get up from my desk and walk twenty-five feet to the secretary's desk and forget why I'm there.'

Edward had gone for a battery of medical tests, including that CAT scan, before coming to me but the tests all came back negative. The medical profession could not find the cause of his symptoms. As we began to work together, Edward relaxed into the altered state of consciousness quite readily. I could see that there had been an explosion, like a stroke, in part of his brain, leaving a build-up of scar tissue and inflammation that blocked the blood flow and electrical flow through his brain. Oxygen, cerebrospinal fluid and electrical energy could not flow properly.

After our first session, I felt confident that Edward would benefit greatly from our work. Edward came on three consecutive days and told me that he could feel my energy as I went through his body. I worked to facilitate blood flow to the brain and to increase the transmission of signals between the two hemispheres.

I could also see that his prostate needed cleaning and that his bladder was weak and needed to be tightened. The prostate is surrounded in a shell of tissue that becomes congested from not ejaculating fully. When the sac is dirty through tissue blockage of body waste and congested as the result of incomplete ejaculation, the prostate gland does not get enough oxygen, causing it to break down, a common problem which may result in prostate cancer.

One morning in June, I woke up knowing that Edward was again feeling confused and I went to work on him at a distance. He called me later to tell me that he'd felt me working. Since that time, he has not had any problem with mental disorientation. He sent me a note a few months later stating, 'I feel physically stronger than I have in years. I know your work had a profound effect upon me. I found my old confidence coming back in a more intense way than I ever felt before. It seems as though my intuition and ability to know grew by leaps and bounds overnight. I even found that my communications with people were deeper and more meaningful than ever before. I know that your treatments contributed to these newfound feelings considerably.'

There is often a personality change when people recover normal brain function and they become more confident and courageous. When Mark arrived for healing, bringing his wife with him, I promised her that she would have a whole new man on her hands before long. Mark felt dizzy and lightheaded. He complained of 'spacing out as if someone is pulling a blind down in my mind. In the middle of a column of figures, I just can't add any more.' I was familiar with that from my own accident – it had taken six years before I could memorize a telephone number.

Mark's electrical field indicated damage to his head area, and when I looked inside his skull, I discovered that part of his head had been damaged by forceps at birth. Because of his birth trauma, he had no memory of complete brain function, and I wondered how successful the healing could be with no memories for him to call on. But the body took over and Mark recovered completely. His whole life has changed, his friends noted that he looked better, and his wife confirmed that he is indeed a new man. For Mark, who had no memories of a clearly activated brain to draw upon, our work made a very dramatic difference.

While I was on a trip to Southern California, Lisa, the mother of two teenagers, came to see me complaining that her busy, energetic life had suddenly become a struggle. She would awaken every morning with a very clear plan for the day, but by the afternoon she was exhausted. She was so disoriented that she once asked her son to open the cooker and pour her a glass of juice. Her confused state terrified her and she had been avoiding her usual activities. The left side of her head didn't feel quite right.

As soon as I looked at her energy field, I knew that her neurology was in trouble. I asked, 'What have you done to your head?'

She looked shocked. 'Robyn, I forgot that I had a terrible fall. My husband and I were hiking with our dog, Wag, and my husband was about to throw a branch for him to chase. Wag went running out like a football player waiting for a pass. He didn't see me and knocked me down, head over heels. I landed flat on my back, hit my head and was knocked out.'

'How long ago was that?' I asked.

'About two months,' she replied. 'When I came to, I stayed on my back and cried until there were no more tears. I felt odd, rather tender all over. But the next morning I got up and never thought another thing about it.

'That was when I began feeling that I was somehow outside myself, but I never put it together with the fall.'

Lisa came for three sessions and gradually improved as I reconnected her energy circuits. The left hemisphere of her brain was traumatized and the electrical system had broken down. She reported feeling heat shoot through her body very quickly from head to toe as we worked. She described sensations in her head 'as if energy had been pinched off and was now turning back on.' When she got home after our first session she called to tell me that she now felt 'tucked into' herself, as if everything were back in place. Then she literally tucked herself into bed and slept for many hours. By the end of the third session, Lisa could maintain her focus all day and resume her busy life as a producer, wife and mother.

I am somehow intuitively linked to my clients, able to keep connected to affected body parts from a distance, and I know when it's time for further work. This is especially true with neurological work. I treasure the tiny nerves in the head. When they are freed from their prison, they react with delight, joyfully stretching to full length again as though they have arms to extend. It's really a pleasure for me to do this work.

No matter what symptoms bring clients to me, I always check their heads to see that they are functioning correctly. In every visit I make to someone's head, I check on two important spots, the cancer molecule and the craving nerve.

The cancer molecule is L-shaped. If cancer cells are active in a person's body, this molecule will be lopsided and surrounded by fluid. I concentrate on draining the fluid. At each session, I make sure it is straight and that the fluid is diminishing. The long side of the L represents the immune system, so I zap this at every session, no matter what the client's problem is. More often than not, with the cells strengthening during my work on other parts of the body, the immune system strengthens on its own. When the fluid drains, white cell heads appear on the bottom of the L, showing that this area is healthy again.

The other brain site I visit is what I call the 'craving nerve'. It is on top of the right hemisphere of the brain and causes craving for alcohol, cigarettes and other 'addictive' substances and processes. When this nerve is over-developed, it looks something like a miniature cobra. During the first session, I communicate with it and try to convince it to give up its power. Most of the time it does so. If not, I reduce it in size. When I have restored wellness within someone's head, I then concentrate on the electrical flow to the brain, making sure that each side of the brain is receiving a balanced amount of electricity. This can only be achieved after all neurological work is completed.

Not everyone has a biological cause for addiction. With more people it's the result of weakening in the mental state, which requires them to do extensive work on themselves. The majority, however, will not bother to take the break to reprogramme that is essential before undertaking this work.

Long-distance contact with my clients can occur before I go to sleep, during the night or at the moment when I wake in the morning. I am often working my clients' body parts in my head, even while I'm exercising, and am able to go directly to specific body parts when further work is necessary. Most of my clients seem to feel my energy working in their bodies. All of them say it feels sweet, light and fluttery. One compared it to dye running through her body. Many can track its process, seeing it as white light. Others have felt its intensity when I have performed an operation of regeneration on a specific part. No one has ever felt pain, although some clients have felt a little discomfort in the days following, especially those who have had intense work on the spine. I do not need to invade any other aspect of the client's life, as I go directly to the relevant body part only. This is a very important aspect of healing.

Chapter 13

Kauai Calls

After three years in Seattle I was tired and ready for a trip to Kauai. I'd been working hard presenting seminars requiring considerable preparation and I'd been intensely involved with hundreds of clients. Some of them had problems I had never seen before and virtually all of them had got better. I needed to recharge and to allow the meaning of my work to consolidate.

Many of my clients and friends wanted more practical help, so I decided to write this book for them and for those who cannot get to work with me directly. Kauai would be the perfect place to write without interruption.

Fortunately, I was able to house-sit for a client. The house was being refurbished and I could hardly wait to see the changes that had been made since my last visit. I arrived two days before the owner was due to leave on her trip, dropped my luggage in the bedroom and without even turning on the lights, hurried across the living room, eager to savour the Hawaiian moonlight streaming in through the windows.

As I dashed across the floor, something moved under my foot. I thought I'd stepped on a gecko and my heart sank. I didn't want to hurt a cute little lizard. Excruciating pain surged through my toe.

'Something bit me,' I called out to the owner of the house. She switched on the light and we saw a large centipede on the floor.

'Oh no, they're poisonous!' she cried. 'Some people get very bad reactions to a bite.' She called a nurse who lived nearby and the woman arrived within minutes, bringing a stethoscope with her. She listened to my heart to be sure I wasn't having palpitations. The bite was beginning to swell and throb with pain.

'A bite from a centipede can be as severe as snake bite,' she said alarmingly. 'I knew a woman who went into cardiac arrest twenty minutes after she was bitten.'

I remembered the warnings Granny Penny had given us about centipedes but the nurse's words still surprised me and I began to send energy to my toe. I sat on the couch with the two women at my side and started to freeze the poison, mentally saying, 'Poison, you are going nowhere. You are staying right where you are.' The feeling in my toe began to change. First it cramped, then I felt pins and needles. Within twenty minutes the pain went away, redness and swelling disappeared and the toe was normal.

'Physician, heal thyself,' the nurse said, and we all laughed. I was careful to point out that I wasn't a physician, but the thought was correct. If I couldn't heal myself, who could I help?

'I've heard you are a healer,' the nurse went on. 'My intuition tells me that you are here not only to write your book but to grow stronger yourself.'

'I hope so,' I replied.

I analysed what I had done with my toe and concluded

that I had stopped the poison from entering my blood-stream by freezing activity at the cellular level, controlling the cells themselves. As I thought about it, I realized that besides freezing out the poison, I'd also boosted the energy in the damaged cells of my toe to help them recover. I was healthy to start with, so that probably helped as well. I exercise every day and eat wisely to make sure I always have optimum energy. Healthy cells have less susceptibility to damage and disease. But I now had clients who came to be healed of cancer, and they were in bad shape.

I'd been able to see individual cells before, and from the very beginning of my work as a healer cells were always boosted at the first session in some way. At the second session I always note that the cells are more powerful, stronger, right through to the nucleus. I didn't know why at the beginning, but since I had begun to study the energy field, I knew that the energetic shift in the system boosts the cells and the blood. I assumed it was something that just happened, not that I was doing it. I made no effort to control it in any way, yet the energy boost they received in their healing was crucial, sometimes a matter of life and death. I was convinced that cancer is inextricably connected to energy in our environment.

I advise that we take preventive measures without becoming paranoid. By adopting a common-sense attitude, we will have a far better chance of combating electrical products, chemical pollution and food preservatives which condition our bodies: it's a well-known fact that in the USA corpses are lasting days longer before deterioration sets in and embalming is needed.

Now we also have diseased meat to contend with and even seafood is in trouble. To overcome the electricity problem a simple answer would be to place transformers at the source of giant power outlets on the planet. If you live within 20 miles of large electrical stanchions, move if you possibly can. Don't become one of the one in three people who fall victim to cancer – that's the count in the Western world at the moment.

It's my belief that most of our anger and anxiety comes from our stressed energy fields, which are having to work twenty-four hours a day trying to keep out invasion of the pre-mentioned factors. Help is available from my website, *www.robynwelch.com*, where you can obtain products for the home and office, such as a wrist-watch, which meld both electrical energies. It's amazing how relaxed these living and work spaces become as a result, to say nothing of the people and animals who occupy them. These products certainly help you to maintain a stronger energy field and many parents report the calming effect they have on their children. Particularly valuable is the protective disc that is available to combat radiation from mobile phones. I believe these phones are extremely dangerous, having the capability to cause brain tumours and memory loss, along with other neurology problems.

Many companies are now manufacturing computers with radioactive protection shields. If you sit in front of a computer for many hours daily, I advise you to take extra care. Nature is a good energy field clearer, and trees are especially effective. Go out to parks and gardens whenever you can. Lovely light music with good vibrations is also a valuable cleanser. Take care to avoid chemical pollution, especially with household cleansers and cosmetics. After a new carpet has been laid it should be allowed one week to settle, with as much air as possible circulating through the rooms, before you live in the space. There are very few chemical-free carpets on the market. If you have carpets shampooed, insist on pure cleaning products.

Keep mould out of air-conditioning units by having them serviced regularly. Beware of certain paints and strippers. Even garden products can be dangerous. I advise clients to wear masks when working with any of these chemically-laden products as their toxins can become lodged in the bronchial tube and lung tissue with every breath, thus poisoning the body. Ironically, it is said that golf-courses have become one of the unhealthiest recreational places because of the amount of chemicals used to create the lush green grass. My work can dislodge toxins from the tissues and encourage regrowth.

Keep your spirits high. Exercise, rev your engine, and don't stagnate. Eat well-balanced food, organic if possible, and drink plenty of pure water.

I have observed and also read that electromagnetic energy pulses through every cell of our bodies. When the energy we take in is different from our natural frequencies, our cells suffer and eventually our health can be damaged. I believe that natural energy runs clock-wise through our body. But I have seen that the electricity from overhead power lines, computer chips and monitors, microwaves, hair dryers, TV sets and many other electrical appliances runs anti-clockwise in our system. It goes against the grain, stressing our energy with its dissonant vibrations.

Dr Valerie Hunt's work demonstrated that the Earth resonates at approximately 7.8 cycles per second and that our bodies are tuned to this frequency. Electromagnetic interference from all sources alters this natural vibration. In the last four decades, according to researchers in Australia, electromagnetic pollution on the planet has increased more than one million times.

Mixed frequencies clutter our brains, which are similar to radio receivers, and the transmission of electrical impulses from the brain to other parts of the body becomes jumbled. This impairs the quality of energy transmission in the field and within the body. According to some investigators, electromagnetic energy penetrates at a cellular level, by entering the DNA, and may cause dormant viruses to awaken and mutate, weakening our immune system and causing disease. I believe electrical pollution is one of the causes of cancer.

Exposure to harmful electromagnetic frequencies can cause other disorders of the central nervous system such as headache, fatigue, dizziness, back pain, emotional instability, memory loss and arthritis.

A month in beautiful Kauai passed all too quickly. I'd made progress on my book and felt that it was time to return to my clients on the mainland. After I began working with people in Seattle, I realized that the nurse's prediction was true: my work was stronger than ever before.

Two weeks after I returned to Seattle a very sick cancer client came in for her second session. When I went into her energy field, I sensed and saw cells rolling. I noticed that even if I wasn't happy with the strength of the boost, I was none the less able to activate the cells into rolling over. I could see them actually turning, as if hatching eggs were being turned under a light. I could promote them into a new roll. I delighted in my ability to control the movement of cells.

Then, about three weeks later, I went into another of my cancer clients to promote cell boost and discovered that the cells had been doing it themselves. They told me so and I also knew intuitively. They had taken over the role of strengthening themselves. I had given them the energy to start doing this and they continued on their own. The cells make their own judgements about how much rolling they need once I give them an energy boost. The client called me later and I gave her a phone session. The cells told me they did not need me. I felt rather rejected but backed off.

Then I saw the process in other people. One woman called me a week after her session and I saw that the rolling had continued for a while, then stopped. When she came in the following day the process resumed during our session, but it was not as pronounced as before.

Apparently, as her cells strengthened she did not require another major roll. All four clients had similar experiences, with the rolls gradually diminishing as their cells grew stronger. I realized that the cells were on their own roll. And each time they rolled, they created new energy, demonstrating that energy creates energy. When do they stop, I wondered. Do they know when to stop? Do they stop because I haven't given the person sessions for a certain time? They would stop, and then in another session would roll again. I was able to get about 95 per cent of the cells re-energized. Now I'm looking forward to 100 per cent, but maybe I'll never achieve that because the client still has free choice. For example, perhaps a client could have an emotional upset in her life and allow that to weaken circuitry in the field, which in turn would affect body healing.

Around that time I began to check the wellness of bone marrow in all my clients. In the past, I had only checked it in cancer patients because it was difficult for me but now it became easier. I discovered that most of the people I checked had imperfect marrow. Sometimes two or three inches of healthy marrow were missing. Instead of creamy-coloured, well-packed marrow, I would find only a few slimy threads of grey tissue in those areas. Marrow weakness is caused by impurities in the bloodstream due to the inability of most livers to detoxify blood completely. Red blood cells are made in the bone marrow. The cycle goes on and on.

After boosting the cell energy in the marrow, I draw some of the healthy marrow into the afflicted area with my energy tool to generate new growth. Besides promoting healing of leukaemia, this regeneration work is helpful in osteoarthritis. Bone marrow can be regenerated as the blood becomes richer. This is not true of the body organs: tissue must become strong before they can accept regeneration, to function at maximum potential.

Then I went one step further. I thought, if I can get cells strong enough in a body, nothing could invade them. Nothing. This was an ambitious undertaking, considering that the average human body has about 10 trillion cells. Would it become possible to regenerate an entire body?

Chapter 14

Heart Energy

Everyone knows that the heart is a large muscle that pumps blood through our bodies. I see it also as a powerful generator that moves the positive God energy around. If one channels that positive energy from the third eye region between the eyebrows down to the heart, it will leave the body via our skin, having nourished and built up our field. This happens automatically when the heart is generating the love energy frequency.

When clients come to me complaining of heart problems, I always see a disturbance in their energy field on the upper left side of the body. I pick up breast and chest problems in this area as well.

Arlene came to me complaining of angina pains. She had been experiencing shortness of breath, tightness in her chest and dizziness. She was quite overweight and afraid to exercise because of it. Her body's oxygen supply was therefore very low. Her doctor had diagnosed angina and told her to take it easy.

In the purely physical sense, angina is caused by inadequate blood flow through the coronary vessels, the blood vessels of the heart muscle. With angina, the heart muscle is complaining that it isn't getting enough oxygen because its blood supply has been dangerously diminished. Although most people fear the worst when angina pains occur, they are not necessarily symptoms of an impending heart attack.

When I checked Arlene's heart, I saw that the arteries were largely blocked. If the arteries get too blocked, reduced blood supply to the heart may result in a heart attack. Arlene's arteries were dangerously close to that level. I went in and gently opened them, allowing the blood to circulate more easily.

After three sessions, Arlene's angina pains stopped and she found it easier to breathe. She told me that she had been concerned about steep stairs to the passenger deck on the ferry-boat she took to work and always stayed in the car rather than risk over-exertion. After her healing, she could climb the stairs easily with no shortness of breath, no tightness or pain in her chest and no light-headedness for the first time in years. Within a year of our three sessions she lost 50 pounds through diet change and exercise which had been beyond her in the past. She wrote me a letter expressing her joy and gratitude.

The heart, more than any other part of the body, is deeply connected to the emotions. It cannot play its role if you hang on to emotional pain. Love and forgiveness are necessary to a healthy heart and energy field.

To maintain a large, strong energy field, feed it with positive energy. You can do this by relaying focused, positive thoughts and feelings through the heart generator. Divine energy, or God energy, is 100 per cent positive. Looking on the bright side, which means looking at life through our hearts, is necessary if we are to maintain a positive energy field. This is not always easy, I know. But because energy creates energy, if you succeed, you expand your own field.

Negative energy has an explosive charge, and if you do not succeed in reprogramming it to positive energy, you will end up exploding in anger, damaging your own field. You must try not to direct negative energy frequencies into your field because this achieves nothing but damage and grief. These negative frequencies will be projected from each side of the forehead into your own field, with a twenty-second grace period. Don't forget that your body can tolerate only one form of energy at a time. We have freedom of choice.

All the evidence points towards pain and illness being in the energy field before it enters the body. As Dr Valerie Hunt pointed out in her book, *Infinite Mind*:

> We discovered by recording brain waves, blood pressure changes, galvanic skin responses, heartbeat and muscle contraction simultaneously with auric changes, *that changes occurred in the field before any of the other systems changed.*

A person can receive the 'all clear' from a treadmill test and yet within a day have a fatal heart attack because physicians do not measure negative energy in the field. I look forward to the time, which I believe is coming, when diagnoses will be determined by examining the energy field as well as the body itself.

A major problem for those receiving massive doses of negative energy is that it creates a gap between the body and the field. I tend to see this gap, which can be as much as

6 feet wide, primarily when I scan drug- and alcohol-dependent people. I also see it in those who have received massive doses of chemical medicine. Fourth-dimension energy exists in this gap.

Our physical universe consists of three dimensions. The third dimension is the material world. Negative energy lurks in the fourth dimension, ready to invade our minds and energy fields if they are weak. People with gaps in their fields become attuned to it automatically.

On a higher plane, the fifth dimension, we find the Divine level of positive energy. A very strong field has the potential to attune us to the Divine vibrations of this higher level. I work with fifth-dimension energy to repair bodies and fields.

Clarice came to see me complaining that she felt physically and emotionally drained. She feared that she had some form of chronic fatigue syndrome. I'd never had a heart speak to me directly, but within moments of going into Clarice's body, I learned telepathically that she had congenitally weak heart valves inherited from her mother. I intuited that her mother must have had heart surgery. When I asked about this, Clarice told me that her mother had had two mitral valve replacements within the last eight years.

During a telephone appointment the following week I was strengthening Clarice's heart valves with my energy tool when I realized that she was not fully centred on the work. She was surprised that I knew there was another energy field present, that someone had come into her room. I finished the heart surgery procedure once she was alone and relaxed again. After several appointments, the repairs were completed. She called a week later to say that she was feeling on top of the world physically. As a bonus, for the first time in twenty years she felt profoundly close to her mother. Their relationship had been a strain for both of them, but after her healing, Clarice could actually feel deep love for her mother. This was a most gratifying result for all of us.

Love is the key to the heart; only love drives this powerful generator. Love is the life-force in manifestation, the God frequency in action. Love is the highest vibrational level in the universe. I cannot over-stress the point: Live in love. Don't block the generator. Why do so many people fear the very food the heart needs?

Don't waste time and energy trying to figure out why something negative happened to you. Accept that you needed it to advance your life programme, learn the lesson and move on. Dwelling on the past won't help you and actually detracts from your energy.

Many people shut down their hearts after a relationship that has not lived up to their expectations and are afraid to love again. If this has happened to you, be aware that these experiences were probably necessary for your emotional growth. Many of them have been put in your path to balance your karma from previous lives. I don't encourage dwelling on the past. One always has to move forward. Past karma can be nothing but a waste of precious energy. 'Accept the past and move on,' I say. If you pull through and learn, you can eradicate negative energy from your system. But if you deny things and fail to put the lessons you needed to learn into your programme during this life and continue to distrust others, you will become hard-hearted.

The notion of being hard-hearted is rooted in literal truth. The tissues of your heart harden when you shut down your positive emotions and that leads to heart disease. The faster you accept the fact that a bad relationship was attracted at just the right time for lessons that were needed to grow and accept responsibility, the sooner you will move on and rise to higher vibrational levels. It takes positive energy to achieve this. Then go one step further and thank the person who has helped you to grow. If your childhood was difficult, remember that you have chosen your parents for your entry into this life. I believe that we have known one if not two parents spiritually from past lives. They know exactly how to promote our growth rate in this life and we chose them for that purpose.

Two thousand years ago, Jesus told us to love one another, even to love our enemies. If you love, you will have an extensive, clean energy field in this bright, hopeful millennium. Try to follow the advice of Jesus and look at everything through loving eyes. You can choose to view the world in a positive or negative way. If you choose the positive, most of your waking hours will activate the heart generator. This will also apply when you are sleeping. Even the dream state will also be positive. Your dream state is connected to energy-field clearing. Negativity creates bad dreams.

Learn to communicate with your heart. Give it full power, with your conscience as your guide. Your heart knows your programme and if you follow it with purity of mind, it will not lead you astray. Keep this wonderful organ happy by asking it about the most minute details in your life. This will give you joy but, I say again, don't forget your conscience.

That warm surge you feel in your heart is the feeling of love becoming an electrical frequency that exits from the base of the heart to encircle your body clockwise. Love from the bottom of your heart, as the wise old saying goes. The heart turns the feeling of love into an actual frequency.

I believe that our hearts have been going through a strengthening process during the last decade and I've noticed that most hearts are now slightly larger biologically as well as energetically. Many of us went through a period of cellular expansion in the mid-1990s, allowing a stronger energy flow through our bodies as we evolved into higher levels of vibration. In this new age, people will live more than 100 years, perhaps much longer. For this alone the heart needs to be larger and stronger.

During my life journey, I have tried to follow my heart. It knows the plan I gave myself before I entered this lifetime because of its electrical connection to the energy field where all data are stored. That might not always feel pleasant, but as things progress you will find, as I have, that your heart has not misled you. My heart always sings now, sometimes even during my healing sessions. I used to quieten my heart when I was working with a client, but now I let it sing on, as it does not impair my work. In fact, this positive energy actually helps me to concentrate on healing and to diminish negative energies in my clients' fields. The client's body loves the music and I work in harmony with it. Many times, I have performed an operation to the rhythm of music, usually a popular song, which I sing silently, as if I were using my energy ray like a conductor's baton.

All major diseases commence with the violation of the law of love. This vibration will weaken circuits in the energy field, creating an opening in the field that can be invaded by negative energy which will in tune break down a body part.

When negative energies take hold in an energy field, this indicates that the person's generator is not working correctly. Our system can handle only one controlling energy at a time, positive or negative. That's why it is important to get rid of negativity. Seeking unconditional love can eliminate old negative programmes and energy patterns. Some people reach the ultimate love vibration, or perfect love. This is the state of constantly being in love, not just with one other person but with the world. Hard work and constant reprogramming are required for a time to achieve the fine tuning that will enable one to climb into God's territory. Most people don't like the idea of such hard work, but the opportunity is there for everyone.

With the power of unconditional love we will not only strengthen our own hearts but also help others to fulfil their destinies. As we become enlightened, we will have a more intelligent approach to spirituality and will accept the life-force more openly and knowingly. Thus will the pain of the past be eliminated.

Two people in love can reach perfect consciousness if they try to keep negativity at bay. One energy field will reflect the other. When sleeping together, their breathing rates coincide and their hearts beat in perfect rhythm. Together they are in perfect sync. They may instinctively wear the same colours, crave the same foods and be linked through ESP even when they are far apart. In other words, they become one consciousness.

Within true love both energy fields flow in harmony, working together to create and maintain rapport and therefore producing double positive energy. In order to maintain harmony, all expectations of how your partner should express love must be put aside. People seldom express their feelings in the same way. Unrealistic expectations are usually the cause of disagreement, disharmony and strife and can bring about a negative energy vortex so powerful that the relationship may have to end in order to escape its pull. Possessive love is very low on the vibration ladder. Jealousy is negative whereas trust is always present in unconditional love.

When we are in love we feel connected to everything. We feel safe and secure, generous, willing to share everything with the beloved. Your love insulates you from negativity. When we are in love, we are connected to the Divine energy because our vibrations rise towards those heights. That glow which accompanies the glorious feeling of being in love automatically extends benignly to everyone else around us. The glow of positive love can be seen in healthy skin, hair and eyes, and I see it in a person's energy field and body organs.

Unconditional love is an even more powerful love. If you can practise this form of love, you will be working on a higher vibration level and you will be truly enlightened. I would say that forgiving those who have caused you grief and pain is step one. As I've mentioned in Chapter 18, the mirror test is a great help. Also, know in your heart that you have tried to support another's weakness not just 100 per cent, but even more. You have then freed yourself to step aside with the realization that you completely love them and fully accept their life agenda.

Don't ever try to work out another person's programme. Remember, it's for their spiritual growth and needs only, not yours. Even if you feel they are avoiding responsibility by turning to alcohol or drugs, that's their choice and that's what we have in this planet school, freedom of choice. Are we going to choose positive or negative energy? Remember that the heart generator does not work electrically if you are allowing negative energy free rein in your life. After twenty seconds', negative energy will come out of both sides of your forehead as electrical frequencies and enter your field.

Unconditional love means just that, the ability to love another with total body, mind and soul acceptance. If you are having trouble with a relationship, more often than not the two energy fields have lost electrical balance.

Live and let live is an old and wise adage. I say love and let live. Your expectations of others can easily transmute to negative energy which will damage your energy-field circuits and lead to illness. If you feel you are operating spiritually on higher vibrational levels than many of those around you, you are the one who is expected to have tolerance, patience, understanding and, above all else, love, with no expectations. Human frailty may be the way a person chooses to go for the best part of a lifetime. Love them for that and don't be judgemental.

Here is some information in case your heart physically falters when you're alone. If your heart stops beating, you will feel faint and have ten seconds left before losing consciousness, so cough very vigorously, breathing deeply before each cough. Do this every two seconds until you feel your heart beating normally again. This breathing technique gets oxygen into the lungs and the coughing movements squeeze the heart to keep the blood circulating. The internal squeezing pressure also helps the heart to regain normal rhythm and gives you a chance to call for help. You will be giving yourself cardiopulmonary resuscitation (CPR) using this technique. Thanks to Health Care, Rochester General Hospital, USA, for this vital information.

Chapter 15

My Views on Cancer

My mother died of cancer at the age of thirty-eight so I wanted more than anything to be able to heal that dread disease. But it was not until I'd been a healer for about two years that I was able to begin. Apparently God wanted me in boot camp long enough to develop my skills before offering these tough cases.

Clive came to me at the age of eighty-five, along with a medical history. He had been diagnosed with prostate cancer in 1995 but had decided against surgery and opted for herbal treatment, mostly with the herb Saw Palmetto. This had given him a measure of relief; his prostate-significant antigens (PSA) had dropped. But early in 1997, the PSA started to rise again. Clive was urinating up to thirty-five times every day and at least once an hour at night, which is 'normal' with prostate cancer. His physicians performed several tests including a biopsy and found that cancer had spread beyond the prostate. The surgeon recommended immediate surgery and set up a time for removal of his testicles.

Clive's son had heard of my work and recommended that

his father come to see me. When he walked in Clive was desperate, though he looked fairly healthy and far younger than his age. He had tried everything to treat his cancer naturally, eating wisely and living an active life with his wife of many years. But now surgery seemed inevitable. Would he survive without it? Although Clive believed in God, he did not believe in energy healing. Still, he sat calmly next to me and suspended his disbelief while I worked on him. He had a hearing disorder which meant that he could not hear a word I said, but his body responded beautifully.

Like so many men, Clive had congested tissue surrounding his prostate gland. Clogging causes the gland to be deprived of oxygen and energy space, making it easier for cancer to invade. In our culture, men are taught to hold in their emotions. This over-control means that they are not able to go with the flow of life and complete ejaculation can be impeded. Men would be healthier in every way if they were less emotionally constricted.

Clive was tired for a few days after our first session but then began to feel energetic and healthy. Then came a decrease in the number of times he urinated during the day, a sign that things were getting back to normal. He told his doctor to cancel the surgery and returned to see me for another five sessions. Soon his attitude towards energy healing work grew optimistic and positive and he became an ideal client, open to all my suggestions. His body parts became easier to work with, his tissues more pliable: they actually wanted to please me. We progressed rapidly. Even Clive's hearing improved, although the ear is one of the weakest areas in my work. Prostate is the easiest form of cancer to clear.

After his sixth session, Clive returned to his physician for a blood test. There was no cancer in his body. He came for several more tune-up sessions. He was still cancer-free when I spoke with him recently, and enjoying square-dancing every week. 'I keep my faith in place,' he told me. 'Faith in healing, in God, and in myself. We can't do it alone unless God is in us.'

Cancer can heal very well if the person affected has a positive attitude and makes changes in his or her life. Clive, with his healthy attitude and powerful will to live, exemplifies this. But sometimes cancer victims are steeped in pessimism, stuck in a fearful vortex of dark, negative energy that breaks down their electrical circuitry and allows disease to control. Cancer is the most common cause of death. Every person and animal on the planet has a normal cancer cell count, supposedly to take over and bring about death at an old age. However, cancer is now being triggered in millions of younger people.

I have found three major triggers that cause cancer cells to proliferate: heartache, electrical pollution and chemical pollution. Any two of these negative factors combined, and the third is usually one of these because it is so widespread in the environment, can bring about cancer.

Heartache is a breakdown in the body's electrical generator. When it goes on for a long time the system is considerably impaired and cannot hold off disease. People have always suffered from heartache but it did not necessarily trigger cancer. The problem is that today we must also contend with electrical and chemical pollution.

Man-made electrical frequencies break down our natural circuits. Our energy fields are working twenty-four hours a day to keep out this electrical invasion. This in turn weakens our endocrine gland system, which leads to hormonal breakdown. This is why there is so much cancer in the reproductive areas. Chemical pollution, ranging from additives and preservatives in our food to poisons in the air and water, contribute to the staggering load that our bodies have to bear, as previously mentioned.

My parents had an idyllic life in some ways, but they both succumbed to diseases caused by these three major triggers. My mother did not smoke or drink. She served well-balanced meals and always took an interest in sports. But in spite of her healthy lifestyle she had suffered great heartache from my brother being born with Down's Syndrome. Sleeping on an electric blanket provided the second trigger. The third was helping my father in his dry-cleaning plant, where white spirits, caustic dry-cleaning chemicals, were in constant use.

My father was reasonably healthy, but he coughed much of the night. He thought it was bronchitis. The notion of chemical poisoning was not understood in those days. I believe that the chemicals lodged in the tissue of his bronchial tubes and lungs where they poisoned every breath drawn into the body. In my father's case this led to a heart attack at an early age. Continual repoisoning of the body causes the glands to over-exert themselves and eventually break down from exhaustion. Multiple sclerosis and chronic fatigue syndrome or ME may ensue as well as cancer and heart disease.

Chemical poisoning in the bronchial tubes or lungs shows up as a dark-looking layer of cells on the surface tissue. When I see these damaged cells, I use my energy ray as a scalpel to remove them. The lungs and bronchial tubes keep gradually sending the nasty-looking cells to the surface and I keep removing them over subsequent sessions until the tissue is healthy. It seems that I only have to dislodge chemical pollutants from bronchial and lung tissues; if chemicals are lodged anywhere else they shed automatically when the cells boost.

With each new client, I check for evidence of pollution in the body. We have a little chat about their lives. 'What is de-energizing you?' I always ask. We investigate sources of emotional stress and chemical and electrical pollution. Life-saving solutions may not be easy. I also check everyone for weakness in the heart generator. If they are in bad relation-ships, they must get out of them or they will not heal. If they don't like their job or house, they must move on, no matter what the cost. Often diet needs to be changed drastically. All easier said than done, admittedly.

Most people are in a state of shock after they are diagnosed with cancer and many cannot even figure out the cause of their unhappiness or the source of negative energy invading them. The powerful energy shift from negative to positive during our sessions can bring under-standing. After our healing sessions, I sometimes suggest that my clients take a vacation to break them out of the negativity that has affected them. A few weeks away can do wonders to free minds and emotions from negative habit patterns. But when they resume their old lives, they may return to the ways that broke down the circuits in their energy fields: the wrong vibrations in the area where they live, relationships that drag them down, and so forth. Cancer cells may thus be reactivated. The count can go up and down in a matter of weeks. If clients are not prepared to face reality and make necessary changes in their lives to lift themselves out of a negative vortex, nothing can save them. In other words, if you do what you always do, you'll get what you've always got.

I can provide the powerful energy boost needed to rocket cancer patients out of the negativity they are stuck in, but I cannot play God. If their programme has come to an end, I can do nothing to change it. Even if it seems that healing is on track, something will derail it. I want to help everyone and it's heartbreaking to reach the end of a programme and know that I cannot turn it around. Physicians learn to be unemotional, but I become completely involved with my clients in my heart. I pray that God will only send me people I can heal, though of course I have learned a great deal from the few I could not save.

Sylvia came to me riddled with cancer that had been triggered by the emotional stress of dentistry. Her dentist had been struggling for years to save a canine tooth as Sylvia felt it important to avoid having a bridge in her mouth. But in spite of their best efforts, the dental work was unsuccessful.

Each tooth is connected energetically to a specific body part. The canine tooth, for example, is linked with the kidney. Sylvia's kidney reacted to the trauma and disappointment about her tooth by setting up a malignant tumour.

By the time Sylvia became my client, cancer had spread to her liver. She came to me in great pain and with pronounced signs of jaundice. Within a few sessions I was able to revivify her organs and eliminated the cancer cells in her body. The cancer was gone, but a tough core of dense tissue remained on her kidney that I had to excise little by little during subsequent sessions. It was very intense work as the core was densely compacted inside the kidney. Finally, it came away. The afflicted kidney became strong enough to work again but I had to talk the stronger kidney into relinquishing some of its compensatory power.

Many of my breast cancer clients have had a hysterectomy. In some cases they were told by their physicians that they no longer needed their reproductive organs since their child-bearing days were over. The emotional trauma connected with this was picked up by the breasts, which are connected to the reproductive system. Breast cancer might be triggered even when the reproductive organs are not cancerous. If a woman has been dissatisfied with her natural breasts she is also a candidate for breast cancer. Any part of the body that feels unloved or unnecessary might develop cancer or other disease.

Maureen came to me with weeks to live. She had already discussed funeral arrangements with her children and had decided to acquiesce to her son's wishes for her to be buried rather than cremated. Her mind was as miserable as her physical health.

I found three different types of cancer in Maureen: breast cancer, liver cancer and a huge tumour below her liver. The liver itself had metastasized. Her kidneys had broken down so badly that she could urinate only once a day. Maureen was in dreadful pain. Her heart was so weak that she wore a chemical heart patch to keep it beating. When the doctors diagnosed her they could offer very little treatment or hope because her heart was too weak to take the strain of chemotherapy.

I discovered that Maureen had been suffering from emotional stress brought about by treachery in her family that had literally broken her heart. That was cancer trigger number one. She had also been sleeping on an electric blanket for many years, which severely depleted her energy field. There was little fight or will to live in her, just acceptance that if God wanted her, it was all right. At the same time I sensed no positive death wish in Maureen, in spite of the dreadful condition of her body and the lethargy of her spirit.

Her spiritual faith made her open and trusting and by the end of our third session, I was deeply moved when she turned to me and announced sweetly, 'I know I'm going to live.' Within a few weeks her cell count was almost normal; her kidneys and heart were working well. Her doctors were amazed at the change in her condition, but she was afraid to tell them that she had seen a healer, feeling that they would not approve. Her primary care physician encouraged her to have chemotherapy despite finding no evidence of cancer in her body. Her cell count was lower than normal. Her heart was now strong enough to withstand the procedure. He told her, 'You never know. The cancer might come back in your brain.' Maureen refused the chemotherapy but the doctor had unwittingly planted a seed of doubt and negativity in her mind.

A year and a half later, Maureen's family situation blew up again, reigniting her severe emotional pain. Again, heartache triggered cancer cells to proliferate. Two months later she was experiencing double vision. I was out of the country so Maureen went to her doctor who found a malignant eye tumour, very close to the brain, where he had predicted her cancer might come back. The power of suggestion is very strong! The physician advised laser ray treatment to get rid of the cancer, though there was substantial risk that the procedure might permanently damage Maureen's optical nerves.

Thank goodness I came back from my trip in time to save her from that surgery. Maureen told me, 'I felt that the negative impact of my thoughts of brain cancer and an additional emotional trauma caused my cancer to return.'

Again, I was able to rid her system of cancer. The tumour is now gone and her blood count is normal. After her healing, Maureen became a powerful and effective speaker at some of my seminars, telling her story to those who might be afraid to try energy healing. In her case, it saved her life not once, but twice.

In another case a cancer patient had had a dreadful childhood with such severe tension between herself and her mother that cancer was eventually triggered. After I worked on her, she felt well and strong enough to visit her mother, who she believed was dying. She looked forward to a tender reconciliation but walked straight into another devastating emotional blow-up. Her cancer was reactivated. I had to repair her energy field and organs to make her cancer-free again.

I could write hundreds of stories about clients whose emotions are responsible, at least in part, for their cancers. When I meet people with cancer, I always step back, take a long view of their problems and urge them to do the same. If they can forgive, forget, and move on from the emotional triggers of disease they have a good chance of staying cancer-free. But cancer will reactivate until the life lesson is learned.

Whenever a new cancer client approaches me, regardless of their previous medical history, I send them to a physician who practises natural medicine to have a Biological Terrain Assessment (BTA) made. I learned about this excellent test from John Walck, MD in Tacoma, Washington, near Seattle. The BTA evaluates the patient's internal biochemical environment by analysing urine, venous blood and saliva for nine different factors. In my opinion these tests — currently not available in the UK, as far as I know — are the most sensitive and accurate laboratory tests available to monitor cancer. I have my cancer clients tested before we begin to work together and then on an ongoing basis to keep a check on the decline of activity of cancer in the body. Seeing a physician often adds to the client's sense of confidence, and I get an accurate computer reading of their actual cancer cell count. I also have their nutrition checked. If their liver and kidneys are in trouble, I often send them to a Chinese herbalist for additional therapeutic support in these areas.

I also try to help my cancer clients to search for the emotional factors that are contributing to weakening their hearts and the circuits in their energy fields. This is important work and not always pleasant. They must discharge the emotional baggage of the past so that their minds are clear and positive.

When I start working with cancer clients, I ask them to come for four sessions on four consecutive days so that I can create the enormous amount of positive energy needed to lift them out of their negative vortex. Then the work continues weekly for perhaps three more weeks. By then, if the cancer cell count is down, it will in all likelihood show up in the BTA tests.

I find it far easier to work with those who have not had radiation or chemotherapy, which cause evident side-effects. I can't begin to describe the anguish I feel when I see organs that have been treated so harshly. I wish everyone shared my love and respect for our hard-working body parts. Organs and glands do their duty, live out their programme, and try to play their role with all their might. If they have been treated insensitively through radiation and chemotherapy, the body must work so much harder, even though it is already handicapped. It seems to me such an injustice.

I look forward to the time when energy healing will be known and practised all over the world.

Chapter 16

Emotional Rescue

On one of my trips to Hawaii, I met a charming older woman named Pauline at a social gathering. She and I had much in common and enjoyed discussing our lives and families. We had a meeting of the minds on things spiritual, especially the need to practise positive thinking.

Pauline told me that she had suffered from severe back pain for almost forty years, since the birth of her third child. She had worked in a shop and had spent long hours on her feet, year after year, trying hard not to complain. Her doctor said he could do nothing for her. Eventually, she had to give up her job but continued to work from home. After a couple of years, even that was too much for her and she gave up working altogether. She had always enjoyed gardening and family camping trips and struggled to keep her pain from showing. Sympathy was not what she wanted, but she yearned for relief from twenty-four-hour-a-day agony.

I admired Pauline's spirit and wanted to help her, but the middle of the party was not the place to do so. She was going back to the mainland soon and I would not have time to see her before that, so I would just have to work on her from a distance. As the party ended I told her I would give her a total healing.

The following morning I woke early and went to work on Pauline's spine, cleaning the calcification from her vertebral column and realigning the spine and skeletal structure. I knew that Pauline was awake while I was working, but in a very relaxed, altered state. She called me the following day, thrilled at what had taken place, and a few months later she sent me a lovely note:

Something woke me up in the wee hours of the morning on 8 April. Over the lower portion of my spine, it felt like something was crawling. It went up and back down and up again, almost in an 'S' shape. I somehow knew what it was and was not frightened. Afterwards, I went back to sleep. Since that moment, I have not had pain in my back. I dreaded the long flight home. No pain. I gave my back a test by carrying five-gallon buckets of water while bending over planting flowers. No pain. I give thanks every day and am amazed at being without the pain that I have lived with since I was thirty years old.

Pauline's spinal breakdown had been caused in part by feeling burdened. She had not had an easy life and had probably done more than her fair share to bring up her children and to provide financially. Most people with spinal problems carry their concerns about life on their backs. Downward pressure on the spine can damage the tailbone and the sciatic nerve, sending pain down the legs.

Calcification is a widespread problem. The body uses calcium to strengthen weakened bones, but when it builds on vertebrae, it can damage delicate spinal nerves and cause back pain. Many of my clients are out of alignment, but when they are in an altered state created during a session, their spines become quite pliable and I find it relatively easy to realign the skeletal structure. The spine is very open to regeneration. Quite often, during a healing session, it will start without any prompting on my part. It starts at the top and works downward, usually taking several months to regenerate entirely. Regeneration will only take place once the spine is aligned with all vertebrae in place, all calcification removed and the electrical system humming along clearly. Like other body parts, the regenerated spine becomes youthful, as if it were twenty years old. Clients move more gracefully, are lighter on their feet and look better once their spines are working correctly.

A client named Wendy had polio when she was six months old and her childhood and teenage years had been marked by seventeen operations and long hospital stays. Polio affected both of her legs and her arms, interrupted her circulation, withered her muscles and tendons and hampered bone growth. She had worn supporting irons on her legs until she was sixteen years old. Polio left her with one leg shorter than the other, very poor circulation, much nerve damage and extreme back pain due to pronounced limping that wrenched her spine out of alignment with every step. Her doctor predicted that she would eventually spend her life in a wheelchair.

In spite of the hardship and pain Wendy had suffered virtually all her life, she was a very positive, strong-willed woman who believed in the power of prayer. After several sessions, I was able to straighten her spine and clean out her electrical field to improve her overall health. She changed dramatically. Her circulation improved 95 per cent and for the first time in her life she experienced warmth in her legs. She was without pain and able to walk without swaying from side to side very much. Her doctor was amazed. After our sessions stopped, Wendy continued to experience improvement in her spine and overall health.

I look at clients like Wendy and Pauline and feel enormously grateful for my gift of healing. They want so desperately to become as well and strong as possible, and their lives are changed so radically with little effort on my part that it seems miraculous to me. Miraculous that they could change so much; miraculous that this intense power comes through me. But I can never become complacent about it. I was to be reminded of this soon after returning to Seattle.

Goldy's legs and spine had been dreadfully damaged in an accident and she ended up in a wheelchair where she spent twenty years before one of her friends heard about me and insisted that Goldy come for healing. Despite those twenty years she was a brave person, giving lectures about living with a disability, writing articles for fellow sufferers and taking pride in the fact that she was making her own life work tolerably well.

A few weeks after we started our sessions, feeling returned to Goldy's lower body and soon she was out of the wheelchair, moving about her house by crawling on her hands and knees to strengthen her muscles. I worked on her spine constantly whenever she needed it, even from afar. I reactivated the few nerves that still had life and reprogrammed those that had lost all sensitivity. I then piggybacked them so the stronger nerves could transmit energy to the weaker ones. In a sense, the working nerves taught the non-working nerves how to feel again. I even rebuilt an injured vertebra with a sliver of bone from Goldy's hip.

This is a big issue – a breakthrough. Transporting matter from one place in the body to another using only energy was a difficult process. It required extreme concentration and I found it exhausting work. But I was gratified at the result. Goldy was receiving energy in her numb body parts and feeling there was gradually strengthening.

Goldy was married to her fourth husband. He was kind and understanding and very sympathetic to her need for special care. We decided she should have a body harness for support; it would be attached to a track system on the ceiling. She would be hooked up to it daily for an hour to exercise and it could help to enable her gradually to walk unassisted. I felt it would take about three weeks for her to achieve this on her own.

I sensed negativity from her when we met with the engineer who was designing the harness system. Instead of being excited about the possibilities of learning to walk again, Goldy was looking for reasons to reject the idea. The whole thing became clear one afternoon during a meeting when she said weakly, 'But what if the track ruins my ceiling?'

This woman was obviously not interested in walking. I had had enough. 'Why don't we talk about why you want to stay in that wheelchair?' I asked, looking her straight in the eye.

'You are right, I'm not sure about it at all,' she replied. At least she was honest.

Goldy was frightened to become a healthy person, frightened that she would lose her husband's support and love. She had learned to rule from her throne, the wheelchair, and subconsciously worried about how the dynamics with her husband would shift if she were a well person. Being a writer and speaker on the topic of disability had taken over her life. She really had no wish to change. I went home and cried myself to sleep, so very disappointed, and regretting wasting my precious energy on her when there were others who would have benefited from my efforts.

But it was another good lesson for me. Certain 'victims' love the attention and sympathy they get from others. It's a form of control. People like this may even be healed of one disorder only to develop another within a short time. They just can't handle being well because being ill has become their lifestyle. Goldy was not the only 'professional victim' in a wheelchair I saw who refused to recover. Usually, people like this feel they did not receive enough attention from their parents when they were children and are attached to a lifestyle that practically guarantees them special treatment. I pray that God will only send me clients who want to be well.

Rarely, I run into a condition that resists healing in this lifetime because it is caused by karma from a past life. My saddest case was that of a lovely little girl who had an ugly facial tumour that made her eye bulge forward. Other children taunted her and her life was quite unhappy. I saw her for months. Sometimes the tumour would subside but then it would always regain its power. I threw my arms up to the heavens in despair. Why couldn't I do anything for this girl? My answer came immediately. This child's karma connected to a seventeenth-century incarnation during which she had been a torturer, putting out people's eyes with red-hot pokers. So in this lifetime the child had been programmed with a tumour to balance out that old behaviour. Don't get me wrong about these views. It isn't always that karmatic body weaknesses point to past negatives. Quite often, a person will come into a lifetime with severe body ailments to enhance spiritual growth.

Very rarely do I go to past lives. Usually, it is a waste of energy, but sometimes it is necessary for me if I am to understand a condition completely. I don't believe in dwelling on the past and think we should try to keep moving forward, taking responsibility for life as we find it.

Most people want to live to a ripe old age. In order to do so, we must adopt a more loving and nurturing attitude towards ourselves.

Chapter 17

Care of the Body

Most people have more love and respect for their cars than they have for their own bodies. They are knowledgeable about the amount of petrol and oil needed to feed the engine, when to have the motor serviced and how to avoid overstressing it. They are better at avoiding breakdowns of their cars than of their bodies. Perhaps this is because the body is free and a car is a costly investment. But if the body breaks down, the cost can run well over the price of any car.

In this new stage of evolution, I believe that the average life-span will be 100 or even 120 years. If we are going to live those years in health and happiness we must start taking care of our precious bodies. When I'm inside a client's body, communicating with the various organs, glands and other parts, they are very grateful that someone is at last acknowledging the hard work they do. They all want to do their very best to fulfil their roles and will do so even better if we communicate to give them love, encouragement, appreciation and the right food and care.

Our elimination systems must work correctly every day to keep toxins from building up. The bowel, however, is often disempowered by what people do to it. Far too many people take laxatives, but instead of helping, these products often cause the bowel to lapse into laziness, only working when help is offered. You cannot take a body part's work away from it and expect it to function correctly. Haemorrhoids are caused by strain. It can take up to three minutes for a second motion but most people are in such a hurry that they jump off the toilet after passing the first.

Although there may sometimes be a functional problem, the bowel usually breaks down from lack of exercise and incorrect diet. Emotionally, colons feel unwanted if they are not fed meat. With lack of animal protein and solid matter, the body's digestion takes place mainly from the waist up. Being muscular, the colon needs activation from solid matter for correct functioning. After a time breakdown can occur if your diet lacks this protein. Meat still makes meat, so to speak. I don't believe that we are ready biologically to become vegetarians. To keep the structure of our tissue strong, we still need to eat a fist-sized portion of animal protein a day, six days a week. This gives us a high form of energy. Most people no longer need red meat, but poultry and fish are necessary, preferably deep-sea fish. Fish from the depths of the sea are less likely to be affected by pollution and are energetically suited to meet our evolved needs. Remember that human life derives from sea creatures: seafood forms a link with the ancient past.

I've observed that many of my clients with colon cancer have tried to be vegetarians. I do not believe in colon cleansing from the outside with irrigation or enemas except in rare emergencies. The tissues of the anus are programmed for exit only, not entry, and treating it inappropriately goes against the grain and may cause tissue breakdown. A dose of castor oil, two tablespoons taken five times a year, is the colon cleanser I recommend. It seems to nourish body tissues as well as the liver and kidneys.

A torso wrap made from wool or cotton soaked in warm castor oil and left on for two hours is a marvellous way of boosting the immune system. The oil is absorbed through our pores to enhance all tissues and glands energetically. As a back-up cleanser, and to keep body fluids in motion, Epsom salts can be taken orally. One teaspoon dissolved in hot water, then added to fruit juice, will activate movement of the bowel. If you travel, I recommend you do this on return to cleanse your system. A quarter of a teaspoon of Epsom salts taken daily on a regular basis can help to keep the elimination system clean and flowing, providing energy with a clearer passage through the body.

Eat well-balanced meals and include some multi-vitamins and minerals, keeping the intake minimal so that the body parts will not have to use precious energy trying to process copious amounts of pills. By taking too many, you are actually disempowering body roles.

I advise adding a 15 mg zinc tablet to the daily diet. Lack of this essential mineral can lead to weaknesses in the body and a decrease in wound healing as well as hair loss and taste and smell impairment. Zinc is found mainly in meat and poultry but because the diet of livestock today is so often deficient in nutrients as the result of pesticides and soil pollutants, we cannot rely on this natural source of zinc.

If you have trouble staying slim, remember a rule of thumb: fat makes fat. We do need essential fatty acids, however, and these can be obtained from cod liver oil – everyone can benefit from this marvellous liquid, especially children. Eliminate from your diet hydrogenated oils and fats which include margarine and deep-fried foods such as potato chips and crisps, etc. Limit animal fat, including dairy products. A small amount of olive oil is acceptable. The right kind of carbohydrate is important in the diet. Two slices of bread can be eaten daily. Many people have intolerance to wheat products, so try rye or millet alternatives. Larger amounts of carbohydrates are fine if you work out vigorously and pasta dishes are wonderful. Rice is an excellent food source. Try to buy Asian varieties or brands which have not had the nourishment washed or bleached out of them.

Eat more fresh, organic vegetables. The more colour the better: colour equals antioxidants. Have five servings daily, rinsed thoroughly and steamed lightly. Ensure that fruit has not been sprayed with pesticides which penetrate the flesh. Do not eat canned and other processed fruit and avoid commercially strained fruit juices which have lost essential fibre. Juice fresh fruit and vegetables for yourself and retain all the nutrients.

Garlic is a fantastic food source as it contains four natural antibiotics that help keep the immune system healthy. For preventive measures, eat it regularly. To guard against or cure colds and flu and infections, four large cloves daily will help. If garlic is taken four or five days running, cut the cloves into tiny pieces, place them in a spoonful of honey, swallow, then drink some water. If garlic is not chewed, your breath should not smell.

Drink eight glasses of pure water every day to keep your elimination system functioning efficiently and to clean the kidneys which act as your body's filter. You don't want your organs to be choked with toxins and water is the surest, quickest way to keep your system clean. Tap water contains chemicals that may be dangerous to the body and 'plastic water', as I call it, from bottles purchased in food stores, seldom has much mineral content. You may need a multi-mineral supplement but be sure it is in liquid form for easier absorption into the body.

Sugar is a major bugbear. The average sugar consumption per person in the USA is now 180 pounds a year, compared to 10 pounds 150 years ago. Honey should be substituted for sugar where possible.

Avoid overindulgence in alcohol as it weakens the body and energy field, as do all drugs. Two glasses of wine a day are allowable, ideally before a main meal. Judicious use of alcohol can relax the digestive system and help it perform well.

Intake of caffeine should also be controlled. Two cups of coffee per day will not harm a healthy, active person. The key here is activity, which burns off the acids and caffeine from coffee.

I have a terrible time getting many of my clients to exercise regularly. I cannot overstate how important exercise is to your health. Most gall-bladder disease is caused by sitting, which pushes the poor little organ out of position and misaligns the bile ducts which are connected to the liver. So stand more and exercise as if your life depended upon it, which it does, literally. Exercise not only stops fat from building up but helps to keep energy flowing freely and is a wonderful way of getting rid of negative frequencies from your energy field. From the actual effort of exercising, you create more energy in your system and help your body tissue to stay strong. Your elimination system is enhanced by the movement and your mental attitude becomes positively stronger. So, please exercise four times weekly.

Parasites can do much damage to the body but most people are in denial of the danger and many do not even realize that we harbour worms. Children should be wormed twice a year. If thread worms, also called pin worms, are present, children will have restless nights and an itch on and around the anus. They will also be fractious. Adults should worm themselves annually. Tablets can be obtained from chemists and doctors in most countries. Natural remedies can now be purchased in health shops but treatment this way can be a lengthy process. I advise a chemical dose because it is fast and effective. Even though I am not in favour of chemicals, I reckon the tiny amount needed here will do less damage than the parasites which can cause toxic waste of tissues, organs and blood. People and pets should be dosed at the same time to break the breeding cycle.

Another common parasite is found in the soles of the feet of people who have been to Third World countries, entering from the back of the heel when walking barefoot or wearing sandals. It can take years for these parasites to weaken the condition of the blood, thereby creating a danger of heart failure. To get rid of these parasites, the feet should be soaked ankle-deep in warm water containing sixty drops of red iodine for twenty minutes on three consecutive days.

Cleanliness inside and out enhances our mental well-being and health. The livers I encounter are in great difficulty today. Being the hardest-working organ in our body, emitting up to six cups of bile daily, the liver has enough to do without the added stress of chemical pollution and food preservatives. I see the liver as the start of our garbage disposal system. It also detoxes our blood supply.

Beetroot is a natural cleanser. I prepare beetroots by boiling them, then peeling and slicing them and keeping them in the refrigerator covered with vinegar. I eat a number of slices every few days. Milk thistle is also useful: any time you need to take a supplement for a short period, get the liquid version or capsules that can be opened and the contents mixed into fluid. Tablets take extra energy to be processed in the body.

Clean skin, hair and nails are essential, but so are clean homes and clean cars. Bladder infections in women can be caused by grubby nails, and during love-making, bacteria enter through the urethra. Everything in our environment needs to be as clean, tidy and sanitary as we can make it. This strengthens our physical and spiritual lives. A messy home is a reflection of your mental state and as long as you allow it to be disorderly, you will continue to be tired and confused. Neat stacks of papers or books drain less energy from your space than scattered piles. Don't overcrowd your space with possessions. Keep only those things with which you have a real affinity.

Wear natural fibres, especially while you sleep, and make sure that your bed linen is natural cotton, linen or silk. Choose natural fabrics and materials for carpets, upholstery and other things in your home. Avoid fluorescent lighting and microwave ovens, which give off harmful levels of radiation. Keep electrical appliances to a minimum; never use electric blankets or heated waterbeds. Keep the windows open as much as possible to allow clean, fresh air to circulate. Stale air is very unhealthy. Burn white candles. The higher the natural energy frequency in your home, the more pleasant it will smell. All this is counsel of perfection, of course, but at least aim for it.

It helps to keep the atmosphere positive if you play music in your home, even when you are not there. When you return, you will enter a pleasant space that is alive with enhancing frequencies. Leave your shoes at the door. Don't put them in the wardrobe with the rest of your clothes for twenty-four hours as they have been in contact with very low frequencies – dirt, that is. It's said that cleanliness is next to godliness. Never put your handbag on the floor. Keep it high because it represents your prosperity.

If you have encountered negativity away from home, leave it outside. If you need to, yell your frustrations at the park, trees or bushes before you go home. Don't dump them in your own space or at any other sentient being. Playing tennis, squash, golf or other sports that involve hitting or kicking are good ways to get rid of built-up negativity.

Take good care of your teeth as well. Many infections in the body begin from bacteria growing between the teeth, so be sure to brush, floss and use mouthwash after every meal to get rid of plaque and other organisms. When the teeth are not well cared for, they can affect their associated body part, as evidenced by the case of Sylvia, whose kidney became cancerous after her canine tooth suffered from unsuccessful dentistry. Find a holistic dentist if possible and get rid of metallic root canal filling material which may set up disharmonious vibrations in your head.

Loving the body is so important. When I go inside a body and see and feel the suffering of body parts, I do all I can to restore and help them fulfil their destiny. All they want is to do their work as they have been programmed by our Creator. When you lie down at night, think about the body temple you live in, and send warm loving energy to every part of it. Talk to it, thank it for getting you through another day, let it know that you care. Conversing with your body like this may seem strange to you at first, but if you keep it up for a number of nights it will soon become a habit. After a while, you will get answers from your organs in the form of small flutters that say 'I hear you.' I believe that if you do not love a body part, it may feel inadequate and decide to leave. For example, I have already mentioned that 90 per cent of my clients with breast cancer had openly talked of not being happy with either the size or shape of their breasts. Such negativity and vanity almost insult the true purpose of the breasts and can create another body weakness to add to the hormonal weakness from over-worked glands which we have already learned about.

Pleasure is also important. Your body needs to be rewarded for the fine work it does. Here are some suggestions for making life pleasant for various parts of your body:

- Eyes: Look for beauty, seek and find love, feed it through the eyes to the heart generator.
- Nose: Inhale lovely fragrances, especially when doing your deep, positive reprogramming breath exercise.
- Ears: Be a good listener. Hear the sounds of birds, nature and melodious, harmonic music.
- Mouth: Taste. Enhance your taste-buds. Listen to what your mouth tells you. As you climb into higher levels of awareness, your taste-buds will warn you of chemicals in an area; the back of your mouth will taste metallic. When that happens, leave the area as soon as possible. I find that shops

selling building supplies and household contents
affect me.

- Hands: Touch. Feel. Stroke different textures. Hug
others, if they will allow you to. Caress animals.
Make contact between all parts of your body and
the natural world. Walk barefoot in sand, which
has huge energy because it is always moving, and
also on grassy areas. Sit on the ground with your
back against a tree to obtain extra energy.

- All body parts: Talk to all of them with love and
compassion, especially if they are sick. Reward
them as they become well, telling them how clever
they are.

If you have a sick kidney, for example, visualize what it
looks like and its location in the body. Explain to it that you
know it is not well. Surround it mentally with love and ask
it to help you get rid of negative influences affecting it.
Believe me, it will appreciate the team support you are
giving it and will no longer feel alone while battling for
regained health. Your love helps your body to ward off
invasion of negative energy, germs and other forms of
attack. This sort of communication establishes a permanent
link to your body parts.

A happy, well-exercised, well-nourished body should
stay healthy for many, many years. You will benefit
in countless ways from helping your body do the many
things required to keep you alive. Remember that the
body of an average adult does an awesome amount of work
every twenty-four-hour day to keep you healthy and
strong.

Every twenty-four hours:

- You perspire 1.43 pints
- Your blood travels 168,000,000 miles
- You eat $3\frac{1}{4}$ pounds of food
- You drink 2.9 pounds of liquids
- You lose 7.8 pounds of waste
- Your hair grows .01714 inches
- You inhale 438 cubic feet of air
- Your nails grow .000046 inch
- You exercise 7,000,000 brain cells
- You move 750 major muscles
- You give off heat at 85.6°F
- You breathe 23,040 times
- Your heart beats 103,689 times
- You speak 4,800 words
- You turn in your sleep 25–30 times

Chapter 18

Becoming Master of Your Energy

Taking care of yourself physically is important, as we saw in the last chapter, but the highest and best thing you can do is to become a master of energy. I've talked about energy throughout this book, but I want to give you a more complete picture here of what I believe about energy, our life programme and the exciting changes on the horizon for humankind.

In order to master energy and put it to better use, we need to understand that life on our planet is a school. We define our own life programme before we come into this school and are destined to live it out. We set the test papers. We decide the type of schooling we will have, what we are here to accomplish and achieve, the length of our days, the companions who will be with us, the obstacles we must overcome and the kind of people we need to attract to help us with our lessons, which are often very tough. We even choose our parents and the ones who will push all the buttons to activate our programmes. Love your parents, no matter what. They played their role in getting you here.

The enormous personal energy field we walk around in is affected by our positive and negative thoughts. Negative thoughts and feelings break down our field yet positive thoughts and feelings build it up. What does this have to do with our life programme? Very simply, most of us go through life holding on to an accumulation of baggage from the past without even being aware of it. We cling to dark feelings of betrayal, abandonment, rejection and pain engendered by events that may have taken place as long ago as our first day on the planet or perhaps even before that. We may be sad because we don't feel that our parents or others loved and understood us; maybe we retain anger because we believe that they did not cherish us or foster us enough. Whether or not these feelings have any basis in reality, we cling to them and they colour the events of our lives, literally adding shades of grey to our energy fields.

If we harbour resentment and bitterness we may have little sense of our own or others' worth. Unreasonable fears prevent us from doing the difficult things we know we should do in order to become our best selves. Whether our feelings of bitterness and anger are based on fact matters less than whether or not we allow them to rule our lives, mostly with unfortunate consequences. Eventually our energy fields break down from negativity and then disease often sets in. I do realize that if a person has felt crushed and diminished in childhood it is hard for them to attain a real sense of self-worth in later life,

You can go for years wondering why you seem to attract all the wrong people or situations and why your health is failing. You can waste precious time blaming others for your problems, shortcomings and mistakes. But if you are to turn your life around, you must take responsibility for yourself and everything on your programme. You can do this sooner rather than later by thinking about, understanding and accepting the idea that no matter what lies at the heart of your anger or despair, you put it there in order to learn the lessons needed for this lifetime.

If your parents or others have caused pain and suffering, try to accept it as spiritual growth. Have you ever thought that maybe you were not loving and kind in your other lifetimes? No matter if it's parents or others, they only play out the need for the lessons that enable us to grow. The ultimate aim of spirituality is to reach into the Divine levels that will allow you actually to love them unconditionally for having taught you the lessons. If your road is rocky, remember that you chose this path for yourself before you were even born. It is not that some severe God saddles you with misery, giving you problems too large for you to resolve. If, and only if, you are willing to accept responsibility for your programme, hardships and all, you stand a very good chance of getting over your negativity and living in the light.

At least 75 per cent of the people I've met will not take responsibility for their life programme. You have to experience everything and you need those tough lessons. If you don't accept them, you are powerless. But the minute you realize you have the power, things will indeed begin to change.

Often you must be driven to the wall and reach a point of absolute fury to get to the stage where you take charge of your life. Anger can be turned into a *positive* to blast you into action, to create the shift needed for change. It can boost adrenaline, the hormone of fight or flight, which is there to protect you and get you out of harm's way. You can't save or change your life by sitting around feeling sorry for yourself. You must master difficult situations in life. I believe that if you have to learn the same lesson over and over again, it gets harder every time.

At times in my own life I might have drowned in negative feelings had I not forced myself to climb out of the emotional pit and remind myself that I actually attracted adversity to help me grow. My mother's death, my burdensome responsibility for the family at such an early age, the accident that almost killed me and left my health impaired for years, my financial problems – any one of these situations could have left me depressed and angry forever. But I would not allow those setbacks to run – or ruin – my life. Early on, I began to use my mirror technique to fight back. It's a very powerful way to get a grip and move forward.

Here's how it works. Whenever you feel your spirits sag, when you start to slip down into those emotional pits, march to the mirror, look yourself squarely in the eye and speak out loud. Use your name and a firm voice. 'Robyn, stop complaining and blaming others for your problems. You put them here, and you are responsible for them.' Or 'I accept full responsibility for the programme I gave myself.'

You really cannot afford to let negativity take control. You must build up your positive vibrations until you can remain positive all day, from the moment you get up until you fall asleep at night. Open your eyes every morning and say, 'Today I am going to have a totally positive day all day. I'll work on this and reprogramme a hundred times if necessary, if that's what it takes.' In the beginning, you may blow your good intentions by 9 a.m. It's hard work to get to the stage of being positive all day but the rewards are great. Within a few months, you will experience great joy.

Even if you are still experiencing pain from your childhood, thank your parents for getting you here and move on. Don't ever try to understand their programmes. It's their stuff. Love them and let them live it. Use all your energy to live your life in a positive way. Pollyanna often gets a bad press these days, but she really did have the right idea about positive thinking.

If your negativity stems from a bad relationship, move on. Don't allow yourself to become trapped because you are feeling insecure about making it on your own. If it is not a loving relationship, let go. The longer you stay in it, the more damage you do to yourself. This is also true of your job and your home. If either of these is not supporting you energetically, leave. You must find the strength to get out of a vortex of bad energy.

Beware of negative dumping by those who are always clinging and trying to gain your sympathy. Don't carry their cross for them, no matter how much you love them and want to help.

Fear is probably the worst negative emotion. I advise my clients to sit down and list their fears in order, from the worst to the least, and tackle them one by one. Fear is the opposite of faith and trust. Divine energy wants us to have faith in it and in ourselves. We will never be truly spiritual until we are confident that we are cared for and that our needs will be met. Insecurity is just another form of fear.

If you fear being alone, then risk a little solitude until you realize that you can easily cope. Once you face it, the lesson will be learned very quickly and you will lift out of the vortex of fear. You will come to realize that it is only a state of mind.

If it's fear of not having enough money, then do without

money for a while. Let it go. It will come back many times over. Greed is very negative. Give things away, share. Jealousy of those who have more than you do is silly. Often, those who have tons of possessions lead very narrow, fearful lives.

If we feel insecure and act like wimps when faced with problems, negative energy will just grow. Confrontation and discussion of real issues are necessary. If you have an unresolved disagreement with a colleague, for example, and complain bitterly to others about it on the way back to your office, the problem expands. Then you pick up the phone and tell your friends and the problem can loom even larger. What an explosion it will create when it blows up, bearing in mind that negative energy always has to do this in order to clear circuits affected in our field! Wars start when people want to get gangs or teams on their side in an argument.

Verbal or physical abuse of others may seem to make you feel more powerful but it is the wrong kind of power. People can pollute their own halo, the energy we attract that hovers above and around our heads. When we worry, this energy is less powerful and comes through the crown of the head at perhaps only 80 per cent positive, instead of the optimum 100 per cent. I try to thrust my worries upward, using energy to push them away with my arms towards the sky and asking God to take care of them for me.

The real battle is between you and yourself. Your soul knows only purity, order and complete honesty. Your other self, the one that is here as a learner in life school, sometimes misbehaves and does not want to learn its lessons. Rather than tackling issues one by one, it races through, often leaving a trail of negative energy in its field. True spirituality takes the long way round.

A healthy energy field comprises many beautiful colours, but negative energy ranges from pale grey to black. I've seen it in my clients, especially in the case of one depressed man who came four days in a row. By the fourth day, the white plastic chair he sat in had become mottled with grey and black – marks of psychic toxins leaving his body that would not come out no matter how much the chair was scrubbed. This person was taking drugs, which are so harmful. Drugs, alcohol and heavy chemical medication can darken the energy field. Next to these, the worst invaders are negative thoughts and feelings. Negative energy can also have an unpleasant odour, ranging from a chemical smell to that of uncleanliness.

Active negative energy until explosion is three times stronger than positive energy. If you cannot clear it out by shouting, hitting tennis balls or even siphoning it off in dreams, it will enter the body and create illness. Most illness starts in our energy fields, coming from disrupted circuits that negative energy has invaded. Every time you have a bad thought or negative feeling you are breaking down your own circuitry. Negative energy frequencies extend from either side of our foreheads where they head for the field and weaken or overload our circuits. These now work back into the body, creating breakdown. To keep energy positive, we have to channel it through our heart generator, as I mentioned in Chapter 14. Remember, your body can tolerate only one from of energy at a time, positive or negative.

Some people spend a great deal of time analysing their dreams. I do not believe this is necessary. Most dreams are simply your electrical circuits clearing out your energy field.

To help rid yourself of negative emotions, you need mind control and constant reprogramming. When a negative thought comes in, you have twenty seconds to get rid of it and save yourself from its effects.

The fastest way to reprogramme the energy is to take the breath of life. Draw in air sharply through the nostrils; hold for ten seconds, then exhale forcefully through the mouth. While blowing, repeat an appropriate word or phrase, like 'Peace' or 'Joy' or 'Perfect body'.

You can reactivate your heart generator by thinking of anyone or anything that you love. This will send a rush of positive love vibration to your heart. Practise so you are able to get the positive surge going within twenty seconds after an upset.

By going over and over unpleasant confrontations you have had with others in the past, you give these negative sequences power. Take control. Don't give pain or illness power. Once negativity takes hold of the organs or glandular system, it begins to have actual physical power. If you focus on pain, it intensifies. If you add the emotion of fear, you feed negativity and pain grows. At times pain does tell you that something is seriously wrong with your body, but for the most part, try to ignore the presence of pain for a while because the body will heal itself if you have a positive attitude. Seek help only if it persists.

Try to solve the problem with natural medication. Pain works by allowing the body to focus on and heal the troubled spot. Chemical medication usually runs down other body parts, usually the glandular system and your immune system. Just tell pain to get out. Treat it as an invader.

Perhaps you have had a chronic pain in your body that has not been present recently. Then one day you remember it and think, *That area has not been hurting.* Shortly afterwards the pain will be back. Why? Because you focused negative energy on the spot and gave it power. Every area of the body has cellular and energetic memory. We need to reprogramme or cancel out negative memories during healing so that they weaken and disappear.

Meditation is a good tool for moving our minds from negative to positive energy. The mind needs to be strictly yet lovingly controlled. It has to be encouraged to save energy so that there will be strength to jump from the three dimensions of earth over the fourth, where negative energy dwells, to the fifth dimension of positive energy which I call God's territory.

You will never experience inner joy or serenity until you learn to control your mind. To have consistent control one must be able to focus in the *now moment* for extended periods. Meditating here creates a safety zone where you can build up energy to soar to higher levels. By stilling the mind, you can transcend the fourth level and eventually create enough power of electrical energy to linger in the fifth. Once you have experienced extended stays in the Divine level of fifth vibrational energy, you will not want to go back.

Practise meditation by sitting quietly and stilling your mind. Close your eyes. Visualize a deep blue light-bulb or blue pearl for as long as your concentration can hold it in your third eye area, between and slightly above your eyebrows. It may float around or stay still. If you can keep yourself in the now moment for long enough, you will automatically lift to the fifth dimension, putting the mind firmly but lovingly aside if it comes in and distracts you. You are better off meditating for minutes with a still mind than for lengthy periods with a restless one.

Prayer is also an excellent way to raise vibrational levels. God understands visualization and feeling. When we pray, it helps us to go to the depths of our consciousness to contact our deepest emotions. This lends power to reach out and communicate with God in order to create a shift in our lives. Do you remember the miracle church in the Philippines where people waited for months or even years for their turn to join the procession down the aisle? By waiting, focused on their desires, they planted a seed very deeply and added an emotional dimension which worked with the pain of crawling on their knees on a stone floor. The concentrated effort they needed to hold on to their hopes and aspirations, ignoring their physical pain, added power to their supplication. This was the perfect combination of elements to create a miraculous connection to the prayer-answering Divine energy.

Short, specific affirmations are also helpful. You can write them on slips of paper and tape them to your mirror or fridge and other places where you will see them frequently during the day. They serve to bring your mind back to the desires of your heart and can be very powerful. For example, if you want to take a trip to Paris but don't know how you'll find the money or time to go, visualize the trip from buying the ticket to arriving. While doing so, add a positive emotion, such as excitement. You are creating everything you need for a wonderful trip.

Remember that it is as easy to think in positive terms as it is to think in the negative.

Anyone who wishes to become a healer should use focusing and energy-clearing techniques every day. You must make sure that you are physically and mentally strong enough to carry the weak. Your good intentions are not enough if you cannot follow through on them. You cannot do anything for others if you fall or fail yourself. You have to be disciplined in body, mind and soul. Your thoughts must reach purity.

The daily effort to stay positive is really worth it for the fifth dimension of consciousness is glorious. Whenever there seems to be a struggle, imagine your energy field as wings to heaven.

You will have the energy to get there if you work to keep this lovely powerhouse bright and free of negative influences. The energy field consists of electrical waves, like radio and television waves. It is brightly coloured, with the colours always in the same order, starting at your feet with light blue, then working up your body with bands of green, yellow, red, orange, bright blue-violet, cream, and the divine, bluish crystal-white right above your head. The depth and clarity of the colours are related to your creativity.

When I work with a client, I use the divine blue-white colour for my energy zaps. The colours in the client's field become more intense as I clear and strengthen their fields. As the field matures, the colours become more crystallized. On occasion I have been almost blinded by the brilliance. Many clients report seeing incredibly bright colours during their journey to the fifth dimension where we work.

I believe that a new era is about to begin on this planet. In the last 100 years, humankind has seen a flowering of invention. We have made tremendous strides in science and technology, which included putting a man on the moon and a computer on virtually every desk. Progress we have made with our logical minds has resulted in a profusion of benefits.

A shift in consciousness is occurring now and we are moving towards an era when the more feminine side of our nature will predominate. We will become more intuitive and nurturing energy will become more important than it has been in the past. Heart energy will take over from the energy of the mind and we will become more sensitive, live and work in greater harmony with nature and become more peaceful and less materialistic. Our actions will be based on love, not fear.

The brilliance of the human mind has taken us to the edge of space and has cleared a path to the stars. I like to think that the feminine principle of the heart can guide us along that path to the future. Both men and women are capable of being loving, kind and compassionate. The time has come to let our hearts lead the way to a more highly evolved intelligence that is within us all, an intelligence which knows that there is a gentle approach to all things because nothing is impossible.

Index